Our Florida

Heritage of the Sunshine State in Stories and Photos

Michael Dregni, Editor

❧

With stories, artwork, and photographs from
Marjorie Kinnan Rawlings, Dave Barry, Carl Hiaasen, James E. Billie,
Zora Neale Hurston, Marjory Stoneman Douglas, John McPhee,
Al Burt, Cristina García, José Yglesias, Loren G. "Totch" Brown,
Jeff Ripple, John James Audubon, and more.

Voyageur Press

Edited by Michael Dregni
Designed by Maria Friedrich
Printed in Hong Kong

00 01 02 03 04 5 4 3 2 1

Library of Congress Cataloging-in-Publication Data
Our Florida : heritage of the Sunshine State in stories and photos / Michael Dregni, editor.
   p.cm.
   ISBN 0-89658-483-6
   1. Florida—History—Anecdotes. 2. Florida—History—Pictorial works. 3. Florida—Social life and customs—Anecdotes. I. Dregni, Michael, 1961–
   F311.6.O96 2000
   975.9—dc21   00-044771

Distributed in Canada by Raincoast Books
9050 Shaughnessy Street, Vancouver, B.C. V6P 6E5

Published by Voyageur Press, Inc.
123 North Second Street
P.O. Box 338, Stillwater, MN 55082 U.S.A.
651-430-2210, fax 651-430-2211
books@voyageurpress.com
www.voyageurpress.com

Educators, fundraisers, premium and gift buyers, publicists, and marketing managers: Looking for creative products and new sales ideas? Voyageur Press books are available at special discounts when purchased in quantities, and special editions can be created to your specifications. For details contact the marketing department at 800-888-9653.

ON THE FRONTISPIECE:
Classic "Greetings from Florida" postcard. Water skiers at Cypress Gardens.

ON THE TITLE PAGES:
Bottlenose dolphins dance a duet in the waters along Florida's Gulf Coast. (Photograph © Daniel McCulloch/Innerspace Visions)

INSET ON THE TITLE PAGE:
Greetings from the "Land o' Sand."

OPPOSITE PAGE: BEACHED FISHING BOAT
A victim of Hurricane Opal's ferocious winds, a commercial fishing boat rests on its side where it was washed ashore in Pensacola Bay. (Photograph © Maresa Pryor)

CONTENTS PAGE:
A wealth of coquina clamshells pave a Florida beach behind a receding wave. (Photograph © Lynn M. Stone)

Acknowledgments

I would like to thank all of the people who helped make this book come to life: June Cussen, Pineapple Press; Nicolas Kanellos, Arte Público Press; Jeff Ripple; Patricia Roberson, Florida State Archives Photographic Collection; Tom Thompson, University Press of Florida; Diantha C. Thorpe, Archon Books.

Finally, a thanks to everyone at Voyageur Press.

Contents

Our Florida

There are few things that summon a sense of Florida like a thimble-sized cup of *café cubano* from a Cuban coffee shop on a humid morning in Miami just as the sun rises over the Atlantic. Thick and rich and scalding hot, *café cubano* is a full palate of flavors as well as a jolt of energy all brewed into one. This is not your ordinary cup of joe.

That tiny *demi-tasse* of *café cubano* is full of symbolism for Florida. The state is rich in history, folklore, literature, art, and architecture, reflecting its diverse population, past and present. From the Seminoles to Latinos, from white settlers to escaped slaves hiding in the Everglades during the country's early years, from Eastern European Jews to millions of American retirees, the many faces of Florida have all left their imprint on the state's constantly evolving culture. *Café cubano* is one of the more recent additions to Florida, arriving with the first wave of Cuban immigrants in the 1960s. Today, *café cubano* has become a staple of life along with Florida's famous sunshine and coveted beaches.

Florida's natural world is just as varied as its culture. It is a landscape of orange groves, never-ending wetlands, beaches, mangroves, coral reefs, coconut palms, and the fabulous Keys. And, like the state's populace, its natural world is also in a constant state of flux, both at the hands of nature and at the hands of humankind.

The stories, photographs, and works of art in *Our Florida* were selected to offer insight into our common history, to tell a universal story through these personal tales. The individual pieces collected here are each significant in their own right, but when brought together, they tell a larger story and paint a broader picture. The tales of our ancestors and their Florida show us the path that has led to the Florida we know. The stories of our contemporaries comment on the Florida we have become, or may soon be.

This book bears no conceit of being complete or all inclusive or even a showcase of the best. There were no rigid rules set for the selection of stories and art that appear here; the authors and artists need not necessarily be native-born Floridians, for instance. In editing this anthology, there was a strong attempt, however, to represent the diverse contributions—spanning time, race, gender, and genre—of Florida's writers. This is a book unashamedly nostalgic but hopefully not too romantic.

The ultimate goal in this collection of writings, photographs, and works of art is to tell a tale of Florida, its heritage and its people.

LURE OF THE BEACH
A youth heads for the surf at Panama City Beach. (Photograph © Tony Arruza)

CHAPTER 1

A Feast of Flowers

"This world [Florida], as a glorious apartment of the boundless palace of the sovereign Creator, is furnished with an infinite variety of animated scenes, inexpressably beautiful and pleasing, equally free to the inspection and enjoyment of all his creatures."
—William Bartram, Travels, 1791

The name *Florida* translates as "Feast of Flowers," Spanish explorer Don Juan Ponce de Léon's description of the region. Léon called the area *Pascua Florida* when he first sighted the strange new land with its profusion of flowers during Easter week in 1513.

The name is apt, bringing forth images of the bounty of nature to be found on the peninsula. Few states boast such varied wonders as Florida, from its pine forests to its marshes, from the orange groves to the coral reefs of the Keys.

ABOVE: SEMINOLE WOMAN AND BABY
A Seminole woman carries a child in a shawl on her back in this photograph from the John N. Chamberlain studio circa 1905. (Library of Congress)

OPPOSITE PAGE: A FEAST OF FLOWERS
Long before Walt Disney came to Florida, farsighted entrepreneur Dick Pope opened his Cypress Gardens in Winter Haven. In the midst of the Great Depression in 1932, Pope convinced the federal Works Project Administration to pay people to build canals and gardens for his pioneering tourist attraction. Pope didn't know a flower from a weed, but his wife Julie did, and on January 2, 1936, the gates opened to the Popes's showplace for 8,000 varieties of flowers from more than ninety countries. A water ski show was added in 1943 as a promotional stunt, and Cypress Gardens was soon dubbed the "Water Ski Capital of the World." (Photograph © Maresa Pryor)

The Grandfather of All Things

By James E. Billie

James E. Billie is the elected chairman of the Seminole Tribe of Florida. A Bird Clan member of mixed parentage, he was born on the grounds of a south Florida tourist attraction and raised in a series of families, both white and Native American. After serving in the Vietnam War, he was elected in 1979 to head the Seminole Tribe of Florida, one of two Florida Seminole groups. Billie has fought to build a financial foundation for his 2,000-plus-member tribe with casinos, eco-tourism ventures, the Micco airplane-manufacturing firm, and other projects.

In addition, Billie has spread the word about Seminole folklore in storytelling and music. His debut album, *Alligator Tales*, won a 1999 Native American Music Association (NAMA) award, also earning him a "Nammy," as the awards are known, as Debut Artist o f The Year.

The Seminoles have a tradition of storytelling that is far older than the recorded history of Florida. This Seminole creation story is an ideal tale to begin the story of Florida.

FLORIDA PANTHER

In Seminole mythology, the panther was the first animal on Earth. Now on the Endangered Species List, the Florida panther's survival is at stake. The Florida panther once ranged throughout the state and as far as South Carolina and Louisiana; today, a mere thirty to fifty cats survive in the wilds of southwestern Florida. The panther has been a victim of the state's rapid urbanization, which has devoured the big cat's habitat. (Photograph © Lynn M. Stone)

WHEN THE CREATOR, the Grandfather of all things, had finished creating the earth, there were many things he wanted to put there. Birds, animals, reptiles, insects, many different living things.

The Creator did have certain favorite animals. He particularly liked the Panther, Coo-wah-chobee—crawls on four legs, close to the ground. The Panther would sit beside the Creator and He would pet the Panther, over and over, across its long, soft, furry back.

The Creator made sure that certain animals and plants possessed unique healing powers. When the Creator touches certain things longer than normal, His powers automatically go into what He touches. He told the Panther, "When everything is complete, I would like for you to be first to walk on the earth. You are majestic and beautiful. You have patience and strength. There is something special about you. You are the perfect one to walk the earth first."

Creator went to work making all sorts of animals and birds. Animals on all fours, animals with hooves, animals with paws, birds with claws, insects, reptiles—why, there was nothing the Creator left out.

When the earth was ready, Creator put all the animals in a large shell. Or something round. He set it along the backbone of the earth—the real high mountains. "When the timing is right," He told the animals, "the shell will open and you will all crawl out. Someone or something will crack the shell and you must all take your respective places on the face of the earth." The Creator then sealed up the shell and left, hoping the Panther would be first to come out.

Time went along, and nothing happened. Alongside the shell stood a great tree. As time passed, the tree grew so large that its roots started encircling the shell. Eventually a root cracked the shell. The Panther was patient, which the Creator liked. But, at this particular time, Panther was too patient. The Wind started circling around the crack in the shell, round and round the inside, so vigorously that the crack was made larger.

The Wind, however, remembered that the Creator wished for the Panther to be on earth first. "We will fulfill the Creator's wishes," said the Wind, reaching down to help the Panther take its place on earth.

The Wind was everywhere. The Wind was the air we breathe. After Wind helped the Panther out first, the Panther thanked Wind for the honor.

Next to crawl out was the Bird. The Bird had picked and picked around the hole, and, when the time was right, stepped outside the shell. Bird took flight immediately.

After that, other animals emerged in different sequences. Bear, Deer, Snake, Frog, Otter. There were thousands of others, so many that no one besides the Creator could even begin to count them all. All went out to seek their proper places on the earth.

Meanwhile, as the Bird was flying around looking for a place to live on earth, the Creator was watching. He watched each animal and did not intervene, but left the animals on their own. The Creator often allows things to happen along their own sequences. Sometimes a thing must happen on its own merits.

When the Creator saw that all was done, He decided to name the animals and put them in clans.

For being such a good companion, the Creator rewarded the Panther with special qualities: "Your clan will have the knowledge for making laws and for making the medicine which heals," Creator told Panther. "You, the Panther, will be in possession of all knowledge of different herbs. The Panther will have the power to heal different ailments and to enhance mental powers."

Creator believed the actions of the Wind were very honorable and noble, so He told the Wind: "You will serve all living things so they may breathe. Without the wind or air—all will die.

"From this day forth, Wind will be brother to the Panther and all living things. When the Panther is making official medicine, the Wind must be there, beside the Panther, no more than a few paces away from the Panther at all times."

The Bird, for being able to take flight, will be ruler of the earth, said the Creator: "The Bird will make sure that all things are put in their proper places on earth."

So this is how the beginning was made. Some call it the Creation. Though there were many, many animals put on this earth by the Creator, all came to know their proper places on earth.

MICCOSUKEE GIRL AMID TRADITIONAL PATCHWORK CLOTHES
A Miccosukee girl hides within a display of traditional patchwork clothing at a southern Florida tribal village. The patchwork of the Miccosukee and Seminole Indians has always been created with sewing machines and did not evolve from handicrafts, according to authority Dorothy Downs, author of Art of the Florida Seminole and Miccosukee Indians. *The Native Americans were chased into the swamps of Florida at the dawn of the 1800s, but as early as the 1880s, they obtained hand-cranked sewing machines and fabric from traders, which they used to fashion their unique form of textile art. (Photograph © Lynn M. Stone)*

The Natural Wonders

By Jeff Ripple

Natural history writer and photographer Jeff Ripple is a devoted explorer and photographer of the natural beauty of Florida, including Big Cypress Swamp, the Ten Thousand Islands, the Everglades, and the Florida Keys.

Ripple is the author of numerous books on the state's natural history, including *The Florida Keys: The Natural Wonders of an Island Paradise* (1995), *Sea Turtles* (1996), and *Manatees and Dugongs of the World* (1999), all published by Voyageur Press. His other books include *Big Cypress Swamp and the Ten Thousand Islands* (1992) and *Southwest Florida's Wetland Wilderness* (1996). His work has been used by the National Park Service, U.S. Department of Fish and Wildlife, Florida Division of Parks and Recreation, National Audubon Society, The Nature Conservancy, Defenders of Wildlife, and other conservation organizations.

This introduction to the natural heart and soul of the state comes from Ripple's magnum opus, *Florida: The Natural Wonders*, published in 1997 by Voyageur Press.

AUDUBON PAINTING OF A FLAMINGO
Noted American naturalist and painter John James Audubon marveled at the natural beauty of Florida during his travels through the peninsula in the 1830s. Audubon's painting of the flamingo not only depicted its glorious plumage but also its ungainly anatomy. The pink flamingo has become a Florida symbol, but ironically the bird is not native to the area, having arrived from the West Indies and the Bahamas.

LIGHTNING SPLINTERED THE darkness above me as I stepped out of my truck into a marsh along Turner River Road in Big Cypress National Preserve. Garish, neon fingers of electricity carved an erratic path across the night sky, some bolts stalking others from cloud to cloud in a high-voltage game of cat and mouse. Frogs yelped, barked, and grunted, punctuating the continuous rolling thunder and rustling of cordgrass in the fitful breeze. There was no rain, but the thunderstorm to the west was moving closer. A half hour before, I was nearly swallowed by the storm while recording thunder and frogs in Fakahatchee Strand. Twin bolts of lightning struck near the truck an instant before the air exploded around me. The first heavy drops of rain hastened my retreat toward Big Cypress, hopefully to set up and record again.

Now, five miles away, on the eastern edge of the storm, I felt safe enough to wade deeper into the marsh, equipment in hand. Nickle-sized squirrel tree frogs were everywhere, calling in a mating frenzy, their plump bodies bloated with air and passion, big black eyes peering up from the blades of grass when I shone my headlamp down upon them. Standing quietly, I watched the needles of the old tape recorder bounce as the intensity of frog song and thunder ebbed and flowed around me. The night seemed timeless. It was easy for me to imagine this place several thousand years before, when the ocean had only recently retreated from the limestone bedrock beneath my feet, when the first cypress trees were small saplings, when no human had yet to listen to this swamp's thunder and orchestra of frogs.

This was a night Archie Carr would have liked. "There are still remnants of the old wild Florida," he writes in *A Naturalist in Florida*. "There is always something. Anytime. Day or night, cold or warm, in the rain or shining sun you can find bits of the old wild left around. . . ." The late Dr. Carr, an eminent naturalist and sea turtle scientist, effused over a Florida most people never see—the wild Florida. He also seemed at least cautiously optimistic about Florida's ability to survive, in some form, the degradations of an expanding human population and its renourished beaches, oceanfront condos, country club communities, and shopping malls. I share his enthusiasm for Florida's wild places, and I believe we can save them for future generations.

Named for the Spanish "feast of flowers," Florida stretches more than four hundred miles from north to south, and nearly as many miles from east to west. The state encompasses the range of 425 species of birds, 3,500 plants, and sixty-five snakes. It is remarkably flat, especially in south Florida, rising no higher than 230 feet above sea level. More than 1,700 rivers flow through Florida, while some 7,800 natural lakes dimple the state's interior, including Lake Okeechobee, the second largest lake in the continental United States. Florida is rimmed by nearly 1,350 miles of coastline, more than any state except Alaska. The Florida Natural Areas Inventory distinguishes eighty-one different natural communities in Florida, ranging from beach dunes to tidal swamps. No state east of the Mississippi River can match Florida for its diversity of living things and natural systems.

What gives Florida its remarkable diversity? A warm, humid climate, due in part to the maritime influence of the Caribbean Sea and Gulf of Mexico, certainly helps. Abundant rainfall and the length of the state, which spans six-and-a-half degrees of latitude, are also important. Because Florida straddles the Tropic of Cancer at 23° N latitude, it fosters a remarkable blending of temperate and tropical life forms. Most of Florida's wildlife is of temperate origin, although in south Florida and in the Keys there are several species of tropical invertebrates and many birds from the West Indies and the Bahamas. Tropical trees and understory vegetation dominate in the southern half of the state, with tropical understory plants extending into northern Florida beneath a canopy of temperate trees.

The Florida peninsula protrudes like a giant paw into the warm waters of the Gulf of Mexico and Atlantic Ocean. Because the peninsula is surrounded by warm water, it has not become desert like many other land masses at the same latitude, such as northern Mexico or the Sahara Desert. Instead, Florida's climate ranges from temperate in north Florida to tropical in extreme south Florida and the Keys, with the southern portion of the state experiencing a marked May through October wet season and November through April dry season.

Florida averages forty to fifty-five inches of rain annually—most falling in the summer from afternoon thunderstorms. These thunderstorms produce tumultuous downpours and frequent lightning. More light-

ICHETUCKNEE RIVER
Florida is famous for its crystal-clear freshwater springs that feed rivers such as the Ichetucknee River in Ichetucknee Springs State Park. This river flows a scant six miles before emptying into the Santa Fe River, a tributary of the famous Suwannee River. (Photograph © Jeff Ripple)

ning strikes occur in Florida than anywhere else in the world except certain areas of Australia.

Late fall through early spring is typically dry throughout the state, although the northern half can receive significant rainfall from cold fronts pushing down from the north. The amount of rain decreases as the fronts move into the central and southern parts of the peninsula. After a cold front has pushed through, freezing conditions sometimes occur in the Panhandle and northern Florida, while temperatures may dip into the lower forties in central and southern parts of the state. Regardless of how cold the north wind blows, temperatures in the Keys rarely sink below the lower fifties.

The Bermuda high, a semipermanent high-pressure system centered over Bermuda and the Azores in the north Atlantic Ocean, has a profound influence on Florida's weather. In late spring and sum-

mer, the Bermuda high is weak, allowing afternoon thunderstorms to develop. From fall through early spring, the location and size of the cell diminishes the chance of rain in Florida by inhibiting cloud formation. It is because of the Bermuda high that the state is not drenched by thunderstorms throughout the year.

The Bermuda high is also partially responsible for the severe spring droughts that occasionally beset Florida. A drought can occur when the Bermuda high expands and drifts close to the eastern United States, creating warm, dry conditions. If the cell lingers and does not weaken, the drought may last well into summer.

Prevailing winds over the state are affected by the Bermuda high as well. Its normal spring and summer position and clockwise rotation trigger a prevailing wind that blows from the southeast over peninsular Florida and from the southwest over north Florida

***Top Left:* Prairie Iris**
The morning's dew drips from the open petals of a prairie iris in St. Lucie County. (Photograph © C. Stracener)

***Bottom Left:* Water Lily**
A night-blooming water lily displays its petals at Slocum Water Gardens. (Photograph © Maresa Pryor)

***Bottom Right:* Pitcher Plants**
Carnivorous white-top pitcher plants sprout from a bog in Blackwater River State Forest. (Photograph © Maresa Pryor)

***Above:* Hurricane Lilies**
Hurricane lilies blossom in a show of brilliant red below the shade of a tree draped in Spanish moss at Susina Plantation near Tallahassee. (Photograph © Tony Arruza)

***Left:* White Peacock Butterfly**
A white peacock butterfly rests on a flower in St. Lucie County. (Photograph © C. Stracener)

and the Panhandle. If the Bermuda high drifts to the south of its normal position, the prevailing wind over all of Florida is from the southwest. The prevailing wind is overlaid on local winds, such as the onshore sea breeze, and interaction between the prevailing wind and local winds influences local weather. For example, in southeast Florida, where the prevailing wind is normally from the southeast, as is the sea breeze, the combined force of the two help push developing clouds away from the coast. A line of showers often occurs where the breeze from the east coast encounters the sea breeze from the west coast, generally over the Everglades and Big Cypress Swamp. However, if the prevailing wind is from the southwest, then the sea breeze is unable to carry clouds inland, and the result is coastal thunderstorms.

June through November is hurricane season in Florida. Tropical waves (large, weakly organized areas of thunderstorms) move off the western coast of Africa and begin their journey of several thousand miles across the Atlantic and Caribbean Sea. Some die out, but others continue to strengthen as they drift west and become tropical depressions (defined as having wind speeds less than 39 miles per hour). If conditions remain favorable for strengthening, tropical depressions can develop into tropical storms with wind speeds of 39–74 mph and hurricanes with wind speeds greater than 74 mph. The peak time for hurricanes is September and October, when humidity is consistently high and ocean temperatures are at their warmest.

High winds (which can reach sustained speeds of more than 150 mph) and flooding caused by the storm surge, heavy rain, and storm-driven waves and tides cause the greatest damage during hurricanes. Islands can be torn in half, thousands of acres of mangrove swamp destroyed, pine forests leveled, and hammocks of giant tropical hardwoods shredded. Coastlines are eroded and dune systems erased.

In spite of the damage hurricanes can cause, natural communities in Florida evolved with hurricanes and recover with time, provided we give them the chance. In fact, much of the diversity of Florida's plant life is a result of hurricanes. Hurricanes are thought to have transported many of the tropical plants found in Florida from the Yucatan Peninsula and the West Indies, washing them ashore with waves or bearing their seeds aloft on high winds. Hurricane winds blow down large trees

WEDDING ROOM CAVERN
Florida Caverns State Park features labyrinths of limestone caves, including the Wedding Room with its column formation that resembles a monstrous wedding cake. The caverns were created before the Ice Age when the peninsula was submerged. The underground world's myriad stalactites and stalagmites were formed from a carbonic acid reaction. (Photograph © Maresa Pryor)

in hardwood hammocks, fostering an explosion of new plant life on the forest floor that vigorously competes for the extra light and nutrients resulting from the tear in the forest canopy. Florida Bay depends on periodic hurricanes to mix nutrient-rich waters and help regulate the bay's salinity.

A warm, shallow sea covered Florida through nearly all of its early natural history. The oldest land in the state dates back to the late Oligocene Epoch twenty-five million years ago, while the youngest land—the southwest coast—has been exposed above sea level for only a few thousand years. Geologically speaking, Florida possesses some of the youngest terrain in North America; even its oldest land is relatively recent compared to ancient landscapes such as the Smoky Mountains, which have been around for more than 200 million years and contain sediments nearly a billion years old.

The limestone bedrock beneath Florida is a product of shallow seas that fed a plethora of marine organisms whose shells and skeletal remains settled to the ocean floor over the course of millions of years. This limestone was carved by erosive forces during periods when it was exposed to air and then smoothed over by the deposition of new sediments when it was submerged. Vestiges of Florida's marine heritage are evident everywhere; the highest ridges were once coastal dunes, and virtually all major rock formations contain marine sediments.

The entire state lies on the Atlantic Coastal Plain, and what land we see exposed today is actually only a sliver of a much broader, flat platform known as the Floridan Plateau. The Floridan Plateau extends to the edge of the continental shelf, beyond which ocean depths plummet in the deep waters of the Atlantic and the Gulf of Mexico. On the east coast, the continental shelf ends fairly close to the shore, while on the west coast, you can travel more than forty miles offshore before encountering deep water.

Florida has not always been a part of North America. Through the Paleozoic Era 600 million to 300 million years ago, the basement rock beneath Florida was part of Africa when that continent was connected to a much larger "supercontinent"—Gondwanaland. When Gondwanaland broke apart at the end of the Paleozoic Era, Florida was one of several slabs of continent set adrift in the newly formed Atlantic Ocean. Florida's continental rock drifted for some eighty million years until it finally meshed with the North American continent in the early Mesozoic Era 220 million years ago. South Florida even experienced volcanic activity at one time when an oceanic hotspot developed where the Bahamas are now.

Climatic oscillation and the rise and fall of sea level as a result of Ice Ages have dramatically influenced Florida's climate and the size of its landmass since its definitive emergence from the sea twenty-five million years ago. During the Ice Ages, the global climate cooled, polar caps expanded, and immense fields of ice ground their way south to cover much of North America and Europe. Sea level fell worldwide. Interglacial intervals, or global warming trends, caused glaciers to retreat, polar caps to shrink, and sea level to rise.

During interglacial intervals, the Florida peninsula was much smaller than it is now due to the higher sea level. When the sea was high, most of the state, especially the southern portion, was covered by ocean. Conversely, the peninsula nearly doubled its present size during the peak of the Wisconsin glaciation approximately twenty thousand years ago, when sea level was more than three hundred feet lower than today. At that time, scientists believe Florida was semi-arid and much cooler. Surface water was scarce. The northern half of the peninsula was dominated by dry savannas, with mesic forests occupying moist sites, while the southern half was covered by scrub and sandhill communities.

Scientists have been able to tell much about Florida's ancient landscape from pollen and vertebrate fossil evidence. According to S. David Webb in his chapter on historical biogeography in *Ecosystems of Florida*, this record indicates that mixed hardwood forest is the oldest terrestrial natural community in Florida, dating back to the first emergence of what is now central Florida twenty-five million years ago. Sandhill and scrub habitats formed about twenty million years ago, while extensive dune systems began to develop during the middle and late Miocene fifteen million years ago. Longleaf pine habitats evolved during the early Pleistocene less than two and a half million years ago. Most swamps, bayheads, and lakes are no more than a few thousand years old.

Florida is especially rich in fossils from the Cenozoic Era, particularly the Miocene, Pliocene, and Pleistocene Epochs from twenty million to 10,000 years

"Profound Strangeness"

By John Muir

Florida has long drawn naturalists to its natural beauty, including John Muir, who wrote of his arrival in Florida in A Thousand-Mile Walk to the Gulf *(1916):*

To-day, at last, I reached Florida, the so-called "Land of Flowers," that I had so long waited for, wondering if after all my longings and prayers would be in vain, and I should die without a glimpse of the flowery Canaan. But here it is, at the distance of a few yards!—a flat, watery, reedy coast, with clumps of mangrove and forests of moss-dressed, strange trees appearing low in the distance. The steamer finds her way among the reedy islands like a duck, and I step on a rickety wharf. A few steps more take me to a rickety town, Fernandina. I discover a baker, buy some bread, and without asking a single question, make for the shady, gloomy groves.

In visiting Florida in dreams, of either day or night, I always came suddenly on a close forest of trees, every one in flower, and bent down and entangled to network by luxuriant, bright-blooming vines, and over all a flood of bright sunlight. But such was not the gate by which I entered the promised land. Salt marshes, belonging more to the sea than to the land; with groves here and there, green and unflowered, sunk to the shoulders in sedges and rushes; with trees farther back, ill defined in their boundary, and instead of rising in hilly waves and swellings, stretching inland in low water-like levels.

We were all discharged by the captain of the steamer without breakfast, and, after meeting and examining the new plants that crowded about me, I threw down my press and little bag beneath a thicket, where there was a dry spot on some broken heaps of grass and roots, something like a deserted muskrat house, and applied myself to my bread breakfast. Everything in earth and sky had an impression of strangeness; not a mark of friendly recognition, not a breath, not a spirit whisper of sympathy came from anything about me, and of course I was lonely. I lay on my elbow eating my bread, gazing, and listening to the profound strangeness.

While thus engaged I was startled from these gatherings of melancholy by a rustling sound in the rushes behind me. Had my mind been in health, and my body not starved, I should only have turned calmly to the noise. But in this half-starved, unfriended condition I could have no healthy thought, and I at once believed that the sound came from an alligator. I fancied I could feel the stroke of his long notched tail, and could see his big jaws and rows of teeth, closing with a springy snap on me, as I had seen in pictures.

Well, I don't know the exact measure of my fright either in time or pain, but when I did come to a knowledge of the truth, my man-eating alligator became a tall white crane, handsome as a minister from spirit land—"only that." I was ashamed and tried to excuse myself on account of Bonaventure anxiety and hunger.

Florida is so watery and vine-tied that pathless wanderings are not easily possible in any direction. I started to cross the State by a gap hewn for the locomotive, walking sometimes between the rails, stepping from tie to tie, or walking on the strip of sand at the sides, gazing into the mysterious forest, Nature's own. It is impossible to write the dimmest picture of plant grandeur so redundant, unfathomable.

Short was the measure of my walk to-day. A new, canelike grass, or big lily, or gorgeous flower belonging to tree or vine, would catch my attention, and I would throw down my bag and press and splash through the coffee-brown water for specimens. Frequently I sank deeper and deeper until compelled to turn back and make the attempt in another and still another place. Oftentimes I was tangled in a labyrinth of armed vines like a fly in a spider-web. At all times, whether wading or climbing a tree for specimens of fruit, I was overwhelmed with the vastness and unapproachableness of the great guarded sea of sunny plants.

☙

ago. Fossil deposits in what were freshwater areas during the late Miocene have revealed chicken turtles, softshell turtles, garfish, and alligators. Estuaries were filled with sharks, whales, dugongs (a type of sea cow), and other estuarine and marine creatures. Many birds and browsing ungulates such as peccaries, tapirs, and giraffe-camels lived in late Miocene forests. Wildlife that roamed the subtropical savannas included cranes, tortoises, an extinct pronghorn antelope, two kinds of camels and rhinoceroses, and by the end of the Miocene, ten species of horses. New immigrants to Florida included sabercats and primitive bears from the Old World, as well as two species of South American ground sloths. The first relatives of elephants also showed up during the late Miocene, including the American mastodon and the shovel-tusker, which had a pair of large, flattened tusks that it used like shovels.

Subtropical savannas and forests persisted in Florida throughout much of the Pliocene even as other areas in North America became more arid. This habitat allowed many grazing and browsing animals to survive in Florida when they had already disappeared elsewhere on the continent. Among these animals were a few species of horses, peccaries, and a type of llama.

After the formation of the Isthmus of Panama two and a half million years ago, Florida experienced what is known as the "great American interchange" of animals with Central and South America. Near the end of the Pliocene, several immigrants from South America found their way to Florida, including a giant, flightless predatory bird, *Titanis*, that stood more than nine feet high; a relative of the modern South American capybara; and three different kinds of huge ground sloths that ranged in size from bear to elephant. Among the many other species of creatures that walked, flew, slithered, or swam to Florida from South America were a capybara, an extinct porcupine, the manatee, a vampire bat, several species of snakes, and a glyptodont, a large, thick-shelled armadillo-like creature. Animals of North American origin also migrated to South America through Mexico and Central America—tapirs, peccaries, llamas, horses, sabercats, raccoons, spectacled bears, and jaguars.

During the early Pleistocene, an extensive subtropical savanna fringed the Gulf of Mexico linking Florida to western North America and to Central and South America. As a result, Florida shared many species of mammals, birds, reptiles, and plants with arid western regions. By the mid-Pleistocene, the semi-arid corridor around the Gulf of Mexico is thought to have broken, isolating many Florida species of xeric or dry-climate reptiles, birds, and plants from their western relatives. The Florida scrub jay, burrowing owl, gopher tortoise, indigo snake, and many of Florida's cacti became relicts that survive to this day in rare, arid habitats such as scrub in central Florida and in a few areas on the Atlantic and Gulf coasts.

The Asian long-horned bison, the ancestor of North American bison, arrived in Florida in the late Pleistocene. Bison survived in the state until they were extirpated around 1800, but a small wild herd was reintroduced in 1975 to Paynes Prairie State Preserve, south of Gainesville, and is growing in numbers. The end of the Pleistocene is known for the widespread extinctions of many vertebrates in North and South America, including twenty-four species of large mammals, two large birds, the giant tortoise, and several small mammals. The cause of the extinctions is unknown, although most scientists believe it may have been a combination of environmental changes and excessive predation by human hunters, who also immigrated to the New World at the end of the Pleistocene some 10,000–15,000 years ago.

Much of Florida is covered by sand over a porous limestone substrate, a combination that does not allow rainwater to remain near the surface for long. Rain is essential for replenishing the relatively thin layer of surface water upon which most of Florida's ecosystems depend. Rainfall is also critical for recharging Florida's two aquifers—the Floridan and Biscayne. The aquifers, underground layers of rock filled with groundwater, are formed as rainwater seeps down through porous soil and rock and accumulates above an impermeable rock formation.

The Floridan Aquifer is large and deep, extending from southern South Carolina across the lower half of Georgia and the southeastern corner of Alabama and underlying all of Florida. Because it traps so much water, it has been called Florida's rain barrel. Its principle recharge area, referred to in physiographic lingo as the Central Lake District, is a narrow region that runs like a broad pucker along the center of the state from north Florida through central Florida, encompassing the Kissimmee chain of lakes at its southern end. The Central Lake District is comprised primarily of lakes, sandhill, and sandpine scrub communities

through which rainwater rapidly drains into the up-lifted limestone of the aquifer. Recharge areas for the Floridan Aquifer also exist in Georgia and Alabama. A drop of water percolating downward in a roughly southwest direction through this aquifer takes thousands of years to reach the sea.

Although the Biscayne Aquifer is smaller and shallower than the Floridan Aquifer, it is considered one of the most permeable aquifers in the world. It underlies much of southeast Florida and is actually perched above the Floridan Aquifer in this part of the state. Layers of Tamiami limestone provide an impervious bottom, or aquiclude, for the Biscayne Aquifer, while Miami, Anastasia, Key Largo, and Fort Thompson limestones comprise the aquifer's permeable top layers. Together, the Floridan and Biscayne Aquifers provide more than 90 percent of the state's water for drinking, irrigation, recreation, and waste disposal.

Fire has been a major sculptor of Florida's landscape for at least several million years. Entire communities of plants and animals have evolved strategies to survive fires historically ignited by lightning in the late spring and early summer. Some 12,000 years ago, early Native Americans arrived in Florida and used fire to clear land for cultivation, flush game animals from heavy cover, and communicate with each other. Their use of fire influenced the mosaic of ecosystems in the state as well.

Many natural communities in Florida owe their existence either to the frequent occurrence of fire or to its long absence. For example, longleaf pine forests are considered a pyrogenic landscape, one dependent on fire to retain its diversity and vigor. In these forests, periodic fires prune encroaching hardwoods that would otherwise steal nutrients and light from pines and herbaceous plants. Fire burns off groundcover and the accumulation of needle litter and deadwood to provide open bare soil for longleaf seedlings and other plants adapted to dry conditions to germinate in the fall. It also recycles nutrients in the soil and synchronizes the reproductive activity of grasses and wildflowers.

SUNSET

The sun goes down over the coastline at Cayo Costa State Park. The barrier island park rests off the Gulf Coast near Fort Myers. (Photograph © Jeff Ripple)

Factors such as the time of year a fire occurs, the interval between fires, and how hot a fire burns have a dramatic effect on the diversity and abundance of plants and animals after a fire. Without fire, a pineland may eventually become a forest dominated by hardwoods, resulting in the elimination of a wide array of plants and animals that cannot survive in a dense, shaded forest community.

Fire, however, is devastating to hardwood communities such as bottomland forests, temperate hardwood hammocks, and tropical hardwood hammocks—ecosystems that may require more than one hundred years without fire to mature. Stability is the key word for these forests, which support plants and animals adapted to moist, shady conditions and mild fluctuations of temperature. Damage from catastrophic events, such as a fires or hurricanes, reverses the successional clock by downing mature trees and creating openings in the canopy. These opening, or "gaps," allow light to flood the forest floor. Extremes in temperature are then greater, and humidity decreases, altering the microclimate and creating conditions more favorable to plants and animals that dominated the forest when it was younger and more dynamic.

❧

Florida has long been a destination for explorers and treasure seekers. Some, including the Spanish conquistadors, expected to find material riches and the source of eternal life. Needless to say, they were disappointed in Florida. Others, including early naturalists John and William Bartram, John James Audubon, and John Muir, came in search of a more tangible treasure—the rich variety of Florida's wilderness. They were at once enthralled and uncomfortable with the strangeness of the landscape and its inhabitants.

Botanist William Bartram explored much of Florida in the mid-1700s. In his account, *Travels of William Bartram*, published in 1791, he writes, "Our repose however was incomplete, from the stings of musquetoes, the roaring of crocodiles [alligators], and the continual noise and restlessness of the sea fowl, thousands of them having their roosting places very near us, particularly loons of various species, herons, pelicans, Spanish curlews, &c. all promiscuously lodging together, and in such incredible numbers, that the trees were entirely covered."

Almost one hundred and fifty years later, naturalist John Muir walked through Florida, recording his musings in *A Thousand Mile Walk to the Gulf*, published in 1916. He writes, "I am now in the hot gardens of the sun, where the palm meets the pine, longed and prayed for and often visited in dreams, and, though lonely tonight amid this multitude of strangers, strange plants, strange winds blowing gently, whispering, cooing, in a language I never learned . . . I thank the Lord with all my heart for his goodness in granting me admission to this magnificent realm."

Florida's wild remnants still awe visitors with their subtle, mysterious beauty, although there is much less wilderness than what greeted eighteenth- and nineteenth-century naturalists. Recently, essayist John Jerome visited scrub in central Florida and wrote, "It was perversely amusing to camp there, in solitary wilderness splendor on a sandy desert ridge, surrounded by threatened species of both plants and animals, within half a mile of U.S. 27—the major north-south highway past Disney World's western entrance."

A proximity to civilization marks many of the "bits of the old wild left around," but there are isolated expanses of protected land remaining as well, including much of Everglades National Park, wilderness areas within Apalachicola, Osceola, and Ocala National Forests, and the glassy backcountry waters of the Keys. The Florida state park system alone includes more than one hundred and ten unique areas throughout the state—ample space to savor the call of a barred owl in a remote reach of swamp or end the day facing west on a quiet Gulf beach to admire what John Muir described as "another of the fine sunsets in this land of flowers." Slow your pace to the pulse of crickets along the banks of a Florida river, and you will lose your heart to the wild.

FLORIDA MANATEE
Manatees are marine mammals similar to whales, dolphins, and seals. And like their cousins, the manatee's survival is endangered as humans encroach on their habitat. These lovable "sea cows" have become a protected species in Florida, their plight symbolic of the state's over-development. (Photograph © Doug Perrine/Innerspace Visions)

OLD PORT BOCA GRANDE LIGHTHOUSE
Twilight sharpens the beacon from Old Port Boca Grande Lighthouse on Gasparilla Island, near Englewood on the Gulf Coast. The light was built on iron stilts above the surf near the mouth of Charlotte Harbor, and its three-and-a-half-order Fresnel light was first lit in 1890. The lighthouse was abandoned by the U.S. Coast Guard in 1967, only to be resurrected by the Gasparilla Island Conservation Association and relit in 1986. (Photograph © Maresa Pryor)

Alligator Attack

By William Bartram

William Bartram's journal of his travels through Florida in the 1770s are full of astonishing passages describing the native land, plants, and animals—including this account of an alligator and crocodile attack.

The verges and islets of the lagoon were elegantly embellished with flowering plants and shrubs; the laughing coots with wings half spread were tripping over the little coves, and hiding themselves in the tufts of grass; young broods of the painted summer teal, skimming the still surface of the waters, and following the watchful parent unconscious of danger, were frequently surprised by the voracious trout; and he, in turn, as often by the subtle greedy alligator. Behold him rushing forth from the flags and reeds. His enormous body swells. His plaited tail brandished high, floats upon the lake. The waters like a cataract descend from his opening jaws. Clouds of smoke issue from his dilated nostrils. The earth trembles with his thunder. When immediately from the opposite coast of the lagoon, emerges from the deep his rival champion. They suddenly dart upon each other. The boiling surface of the lake marks their rapid course, and a terrific conflict commences. They now sink to the bottom folded together in horrid wreaths. The water becomes thick and discoloured. Again they rise, their jaws clap together, re-echoing through the deep surrounding forests. Again they sink, when the contest ends at the muddy bottom of the lake, and the vanquished makes a hazardous escape, hiding himself in the muddy turbulent waters and sedge on a distant shore. The proud victor exulting returns to the place of action. The shores and forests resound his dreadful roar, together with the triumphing shouts of the plaited tribes around, witnesses of the horrid combat.

My apprehensions were highly alarmed after being a spectator of so dreadful a battle. It was obvious that every delay would but tend to increase my dangers and difficulties, as the sun was near setting, and the alligators gathered around my harbour from all quarters. From these considerations I concluded to be expeditious in my trip to the lagoon, in order to take some fish. Not thinking it prudent to take my fusee with me, lest I might lose it overboard in case of a battle, which I had every reason to dread before my return, I therefore furnished myself with a club for my defence, went on board, and penetrating the first line of those which surrounded my harbour, they gave way; but being pursued by several very large ones, I kept strictly on the watch, and paddled with all my might towards the entrance of the lagoon, hoping to be sheltered there from the multitude of my assailants; but ere I had half-way reached the place, I was attacked on all sides, several endeavouring to overset the canoe. My situation now became precarious to the last degree: two very large ones attacked me closely, at the same instant, rushing up with their heads and part of their bodies above the water, roaring terribly and belching floods of water over me. They struck their jaws together so close to my ears, as almost to stun me, and I expected every moment to be dragged out of the boat and instantly devoured. But I applied my weapons so effectually about me, though at random, that I was so successful as to beat them off a little; when, finding that they designed to renew the battle, I made for the shore, as the only means left me for my preservation; for, by keeping close to it, I should have my enemies on one side of me only, whereas I was before surrounded by them; and there was a probability, if pushed to the last extremity, of saving myself, by jumping out of the canoe on shore, as it is easy to outwalk them on land, although comparatively as swift as lightning in the water. I found this last expedient alone could fully answer my expectations, for as soon as I gained the shore, they drew off and kept aloof. This was a happy relief, as my confidence was, in some degree, recovered by it. On recollecting myself, I discovered that I had almost reached the entrance of the lagoon, and determined to venture in, if possible, to take a few fish, and then return to my harbour, while day-light continued; for I could now, with caution and resolution, make my way with safety along shore; and indeed there was no other way to regain my camp, without leaving my boat and making my retreat through the marshes and reeds, which, if I could even effect, would have been in a manner throwing myself away, for then there would have been no hopes of ever recovering my bark, and returning in safety to any settlements of men. I accordingly proceeded, and made good my entrance into the lagoon, though not without opposition from the alligators, who formed a line across the entrance, but did not pursue me into it, nor was I molested by any there, though there were some very large ones in a cove at the upper end. I soon caught more trout than I had present occasion for, and the air was too hot and sultry to admit of their being kept for many hours, even though salted or barbecued. I now prepared for my return to camp, which I succeeded in with but little trouble, by keeping close to the shore; yet I was opposed upon re-entering the river out of the lagoon, and pursued near to my landing (though not closely attacked), particularly by an old daring one, about twelve feet in length, who kept close after me; and when I stepped on shore and turned about, in order to draw up my canoe, he rushed up near my feet, and lay there for some time, looking me in the face, his head and shoulders out of water. I resolved he should pay for his temerity, and having a heavy load in my fusee, I ran to my camp, and returning with my piece, found him with his foot on the gunwale of the boat, in search of fish. On my coming up he withdrew sullenly and slowly into the water, but soon returned and placed himself in his former position, looking at me, and seeming neither fearful nor any way disturbed. I soon dispatched him by lodging the contents of my gun in his head, and then proceeded to cleanse and prepare my fish for supper; and accordingly took them out of the boat, laid them down on the sand close to the water, and began to scale them; when, raising my head, I saw before me, through the clear water, the head and shoulders of a very large alligator, moving slowly towards me. I instantly stepped back, when, with a sweep of his tail, he brushed off several of my fish. It was certainly most providential that I looked up at that instant, as the monster would probably, in less than a minute, have seized and dragged me into the river. This incredible boldness of the animal disturbed me greatly, supposing there could now be no reasonable safety for me during the night, but by keeping continually on the watch: I therefore, as soon as I had prepared the fish, proceeded to secure myself and effects in the best Manner I could. In the first place, I hauled my bark upon the shore, almost clear out of the water, to prevent their oversetting or sinking her; after this, every moveable was taken out and carried to my camp, which was but a few yards off; then ranging some dry wood in such order as was the most convenient, I cleared the ground round about it, that there might be no impediment in my way, in case of an attack in the night, either from the water or the land; for I discovered by this time, that this small isthmus, from its remote situation and fruitfulness, was resorted to by bears and wolves. Having prepared myself in the best manner I could, I charged my gun, and proceeded to reconnoitre my camp and the adjacent grounds; when I discovered that the peninsula and grove, at the distance of about two hundred yards from my encampment, on the land side, were invested by a cypress swamp, covered with water, which below was joined to the shore of the little lake, and above to the marshes surrounding the lagoon; so that I was confined to an islet exceedingly circumscribed) and I found there was no other retreat for me, in case of an attack, but by either ascending one of the large oaks, or pushing off with my boat.

It was by this time dusk, and the alligators had nearly ceased their roar, when I was again alarmed by a tumultuous noise that seemed to be in my harbour, and therefore engaged my immediate attention. Returning to my camp, I found it undisturbed, and then continued on to the extreme point of the promontory, where I saw a scene, new and surprising, which at first threw my senses into such a tumult, that it was some time before I could comprehend what was the matter; however, I soon accounted for the prodigious assemblage of crocodiles at this place, which exceeded every thing of the kind I had ever heard of.

How shall I express myself so as to convey an adequate idea of it to the reader, and at the same time avoid raising suspicions of my veracity? Should I say that the river (in this place) from shore to shore, and perhaps near half a mile above and below me, appeared to be one solid bank of fish, of various kinds, pushing through this narrow pass of St. Juan's into the little lake, on their return down the river, and that the alligators were in such incredible numbers, and so close together from shore to shore, that it would have been easy to have walked across on their heads, had the animals been harmless? What expressions can sufficiently declare the shocking scene that for some minutes continued, whilst this mighty army of fish were forcing the pass? During this attempt, thousands, I may say hundreds of thousands, of them were caught and swallowed by the devouring alligators. I have seen an alligator take up out of the water several great fish at a time, and just squeeze them betwixt his jaws, while the tails of the great trout flapped about his eyes and lips, ere he had swallowed them. The horrid noise of their closing jaws, their plunging amidst the broken banks of fish, and rising with their prey some feet upright above the water, the floods of water and blood rushing out of their mouths, and the clouds of vapour issuing from their wide nostrils, were truly frightful. This scene continued at intervals during the night, as the fish came to the pass. After this sight, shocking and tremendous as it was, I found myself somewhat easier and more reconciled to my situation; being convinced that their extraordinary assemblage here was owing to the annual feast of fish; and that they were so well employed in their own element, that I had little occasion to fear their paying me a visit.

❧

The Florida Keys

By Joy Williams

For a novelist and short story writer to turn her hand to compiling a guidebook hints at a great love for her subject. Joy Williams is well known for her novels *State of Grace* (1973), *The Changeling* (1978), and *Breaking and Entering* (1988), and her short stories have appeared in numerous magazines, literary journals, and the collections *Taking Care* (1982) and *Escapes* (1990).

Her fascination with Florida and especially the Keys surfaces in *The Florida Keys: A History and Guide* (1987), a travel guide that is full of literary and even poetic descriptions and anecdotes. As *Condé Naste Traveler* magazine simply stated, it is "one of the best guidebooks ever written."

Williams was born in Massachusetts but moved to Sarasota in 1965 to work as a researcher for a marine laboratory. She has since made the Keys her home.

Great White Heron
A great white heron scans the incoming Atlantic surf for fish at Bahia Honda State Park in the Keys. (Photograph © Robb Helfrick)

THE FLORIDA KEYS do not run due south. They drift southwest, Route 1 running more east–west than north–south. The Gulf side is actually Florida Bay, the upper reaches of which belong to the Everglades. The bay side is called the "back country" or "outback." The Atlantic side is actually the Straits of Florida, where wide Hawk Channel runs out from shore to the reef, which stretches the length of the Keys. Beyond the reef is the Gulf Stream—"out front"—that great oceanic river whose demarcation is clearly seen, the water being a profound and fabulous blue. Beyond the Gulf Stream lies, then, the ocean.

The Keys run from Biscayne Bay to the Dry Tortugas, a distance of some 180 miles. No road runs to the keys north of Key Largo—Sands, Elliott, and Old Rhodes—and the Tortugas are 70 watery, wild miles from Key West. The distance accessible by car is some 106 miles—from Key Largo to Key West. That road, originally built in the 1930s, replaced Henry Flagler's Florida East Coast Extension railroad line, an amazing piece of engineering which had linked the Keys since 1912 and which was destroyed by a hurricane in 1935. The Mile Markers . . .—green signs with white numerals, posted on the right-hand shoulder—were first placed along the Keys by the railroad.

On a map, the Keys look fairly improbable—and Route 1, the line that drops down their sprinkled length, improbable too. The possibilities are vast, but the road itself is simple, which explains why some travelers begin at Key Largo, hang onto the steering wheel, and don't stop until Key West, heeding the billboards' urging, Go All the Way, with all its attendant, randy implications of reckless fulfillment. Other travelers arrive in the Keys, love them, stick close to Islamorada, and wouldn't dream of going all the way, considering Key West weird, if not bizarre, as though that singular and raffish place was at the bottom of an ever-darkening well.

But of course the Keys don't really go from light to dark. The Keys sparkle downward, warm and bright, full of light and air and a bit of intrigue. The Keys are relaxed, a little reckless. The Keys are water and sky, horizon, daybreak, spectacular sunsets, the cup of night. The least interesting thing about them is the road, but the road, as is its nature, allows entrance. The road is the beginning.

There are some automobile guides, such as the old Sanborn Guides to Mexico, that are wonderfully jit-tery backseat companions, not pointing out cathedrals and markets (because the route in question is manifestly lacking in cathedrals and markets), but taking great pains to point out everything else. A child selling an iguana is *here;* half a kilometer down the road you will pass a most peculiarly shaped boulder; a bit beyond that there was once a Pemex station, though unfortunately, a Pemex station is no longer there, only a tire dump; two kilometers away the road curves. . . . And so on.

The Keys once lent themselves to this sort of innocent treatment, and in a way they still do. There is the road, and there are the dutiful descending markers accompanying your every mile, suggesting that a trip is little more than coloring your own experience between provided lines. At MM #— there is an egret; at MM #— there's a pretty view between two violet jacaranda trees; at MM #—, if you can wait that long, is a bar where the bartender wears live snakes wrapped around her neck and wrists—her "pretties," she calls them. . . . And so on.

Time passes, of course. The snake lady is run over one night as she is crossing the road. Someone builds his dream house in front of the pretty view, cutting down the jacaranda trees in the process. But the Keys, though no longer the empty, silent stretches they once were, still markedly lack (you might as well be told) historical and cultural monuments. And the osprey still builds his nest larger each year at MM #—. And the tarpon still roll and flash each spring under the bridge at MM #—. And certainly at MM #— the disreputable bar remains. The best way to enjoy the Keys is still to seek out their simplicity and their eccentricity.

The Keys have been largely ignored until recently, the lack of fresh water being the real inhibitor to development. The Navy had built an 18-inch pipeline in 1942 that ran the 130 miles from the Everglades wells in Florida City to Key West. The water took a week to travel the route. In 1982 the old pipe was replaced with a 36-inch pipe, increasing the quantity fourfold, providing indeed an oversupply of water and accelerating building and population growth. Oddly, the pipeline, as well as the construction of new bridges and wider roads, took place seven years after the state had designated Monroe County, which is the Keys, an "area of critical state concern" in an attempt to slow development (a perfectly nice word that unfortunately has

FORT JEFFERSON
Nicknamed the "Gibraltar of the Gulf," Fort Jefferson on Garden Key in the Dry Tortugas appears impregnable but was in fact rarely used. Construction started in 1846; thirty years later, the hexagonal fort still was not complete. Federal troops occupied it briefly during the Civil War, and it later served as a prison. (Photograph © Tony Arruza)

SLOPPY JOE'S BAR
A Key West landmark, Sloppy Joe's Bar glows beneath its lurid neon canopy. Under an earlier moniker, the bar was a hangout of writer Ernest Hemingway, who called Key West home for many years. (Photograph © Robb Helfrick)

been stolen away—undoubtedly while we were not looking—by the developers). A peculiar event occurred recently. Realtors dressed up in wood rat costumes and organized motorcades and rallies to protest new state guidelines that would restrict development in the Keys. It is true. People who felt themselves endangered by environmental laws dressed up like the cotton mouse and the wood rat—present inhabitants of mangrove swamp and hammock—and, aroused by lawyers and politicians, made a long, noisy trip down the highway to Key West, where the governor was speaking, picking up additional incensed rat- and mouse-garbed people along the way. This is typical oddball Keys, but in this case, peculiarity has a threateningly modern and consumptive edge, which is familiarly Floridian.

W. C. Barron, the founder of Wall Street's *Barron's*

magazine, said early in this century that the only values in the state of Florida are the values created by man. This was how the state was perceived by the wealthy who came from elsewhere to exploit it. Florida, that splendid, subtle, once fabulous state, has been exploited, miscomprehended and misused, drained and diked, filled in and paved over. The values of man have been imposed with a vengeance.

Half of the historic Everglades is now farms, groves, and cities, and this marvelous ecosystem isn't working anymore. Over the last 50 years, 90 percent of the 'glades' wading-bird population has been lost. To read the roll of its endangered species is heartbreaking. The reef is becoming increasingly stressed by sewage that flows quickly through the porous rock of the Keys and into the ocean, as well as by agricultural runoff from the mainland that gets dumped into Florida

Bay from the Everglades.

The bill is coming. It's not like the bill from a wonderful restaurant, *Louie's*, for example. It's not the bill for the lovely fresh snapper, the lovely wines, the lovely brownie with bourbon ice cream and caramel sauce at the lovely table beside the lovely sea. It's the bill for all our environmental mistakes of the past. The big bill.

"Keys" comes from the Spanish word *cayos*, for "little islands." The Keys are little, and they are fragile. They cannot sustain any more "dream houses" or "dream resorts." The sustaining dream is in the natural world—the world that each of us should respect, enjoy, and protect so that it may be enjoyed again—the world to which one can return and be refreshed.

Time passes. There are more of the many, and they want too much. What the traveler wants, of course, is not development but adventure, and this is still possible in the Keys. The Keys have always been different. May they remain that way. Here's to them.

❧

The Spanish first found the Keys in Ponce de León's 1513 expedition and promptly called them, with inquisitional flair, *Los Martires*—the martyrs—because they seemed twisted and tortured. They logged out the mahogany that grew here early on, and probably enslaved the native Caloosa Indians, but they were indifferent to exploring or settling these stony islands. There was no gold, no fresh water, and many, many bugs. They mapped and named the Keys principally as an aid to their ships, which, laden with gold and silver, used the Florida Straits as their route from the New World back to the Old.

The first settlement in the Keys was at *Cayo Hueso*, or Key West, in 1822, more than two decades before Florida became a state. The other keys remained pretty much deserted until 1874, when the government surveyed them and plotted land for homesteading. The early homes were primitive, built from the local "coastal store"—the beach—with wood and materials washed up from shipwrecks. The biggest plague of the settlers was mosquitoes. The mosquito was king of the Keys. Mosquitoes blackened the sides of houses and obscured the shapes of animals. Mosquitoes blackened the cheesecloth which people swathed their heads in as they slept. If you swung a pint cup, the saying went, you'd come up with a quart full of mosquitoes. Smudgepots burned constantly inside and outside the

KEY LARGO
Florida boasts a starring role as a birthplace of modern detective fiction and noir *writing. In the 1948 celluloid classic* Key Largo *directed by John Huston, Humphrey Bogart, Lauren Bacall, and Edward G. Robinson fought a war of wits under the threat of a hurricane. Genre father John D. MacDonald's famous Travis McGee series sold millions of books and inspired many other mystery writers, including Carl Hiaasen. And although he hailed from Detroit, Elmore Leonard's best thrillers take place in Florida and beat with the pulse of the state's heart.*

driftwood houses. Burlap bags filled with wood chips soaked in old engine oil were hung to drip over stagnant water holes in an attempt to kill mosquito larvae. With mosquitoes gnawing on them day and night, a few pioneering families nevertheless managed to claw a living from what one writer of the time referred to as "worthless, chaotic fragments of coral reef, limestone and mangrove swamp."

The people who first made their homes in the Upper Keys were hardworking Methodist fishermen and farmers. They spoke with a Cockney accent, were closely interrelated, and bore the names Albury, Pinder, Johnson, Russell, and Lowe. Their more flamboyant wrecking neighbors were in Key West, but life in the "outside keys" was earnestly drab, farming rock being

THE RAREFIED BLUE OF THE KEYS WATER
The glorious aqua-blue waters of the Keys draw snorkelers from around the world. Here, a diver swims near the old Molasses Reef lighthouse in the Florida Keys National Marine Sanctuary off Key Largo. (Photograph © Doug Perrine/Innerspace Visions)

somewhat Sisyphian in nature. But farm the rock they did, burning and clearing the land and planting coconuts, citrus, pineapple, and melons in the ashy interstices between the coral. They homesteaded on the Atlantic, and transportation between the scattered houses was by shallow-draft boat. These boats also took the produce out to deeper waters, where it was off-loaded onto schooners which sailed to Key West as well as to northern ports.

In 1905, Henry Flagler, a former partner of John D. Rockefeller in Standard Oil and president of the Florida East Coast Railroad, began extending the train track from Homestead, through the Everglades to Key Largo. Flagler was always pushing southward, legend has it, because his wives were forever wanting to be warmer. That is why he pushed down from St. Augustine to Palm Beach. (Flagler also altered Florida history by having the state's strict divorce laws changed when an early wife of his went mad.) But the reason he desired the terminus of his Florida railroad to be in Key West was because it was a fine deep-water port. Shipping out of Miami was limited by the 12-foot depth of Biscayne Bay. Flagler was seventy-five years old when construction started and died only a few months after the project was completed in 1912.

For seven years, the track and train, freighted with peril and mishap, inched their way down the Keys to Key West. Settlers in the Upper Keys longed for the railroad to be completed, believing that it would put them in closer touch with their markets and make them wealthy. But eventually the railroad meant the end of their little coastal communities and their large fruit farms. Key West became a receiving center for produce from all over the Caribbean and South America, and cheaper fruit was introduced to the mainland. Too, the few inches of Keys' topsoil that had supported such exotics as Porto Rico, Abbakka Queen, and Sugar Loaf pineapples was soon robbed of all nutrients, and the plantations failed. Towns like Planter, which once shipped out a million crates of limes, pineapples, tomatoes, and melons a year by schooner, simply disappeared, a victim of sporadic hurricanes and the railroad. Other communities that sprang up along the track vanished too, when the 1935 hurricane blew the train away.

It was this hurricane—*the* hurricane, the nameless one—that made the history of the Upper Keys. It swept across the Matecumbe Keys on September 2,

1935, with an 18-foot tidal wave and 200-mph winds. Matecumbe is a name of obscure origins, but it may be a corruption of the Spanish *mata hombre*—"kill man"—which was also the meaning of Cuchiyaga, the Indian name for the island. In any case, it was a fated place. More than eight hundred people died in the hurricane, many of them members of the second "Bonus Army" of World War I veterans who, seeking early military benefits, had been hired instead by the Federal Emergency Relief Administration for work projects across the country. In this instance, they were building a road from Lower Matecumbe to Grassy Key so that the ferry route could be eliminated. Most of them died when the train sent down to rescue them was blown off the tracks in Islamorada. Of the eleven cars, only the 106-ton locomotive, "Old 447," remained upright, saving the lives of the engineer and the fireman. Many of the dead were burned in funeral pyres overseen by the National Guard in the sunny days after the storm, while others were buried in a common crypt marked by a monument in Islamorada.

Besides winds, the history here is in the waters—in the wrecks and reefs. The waters off the Upper Keys conceal a remarkable number of wrecks, from Spanish galleons to British frigates to World War II freighters. Cannon from the HMS *Winchester*, a 60-gun British frigate which went down in a hurricane in 1695, are displayed on dry ground at Pennecamp Park, and the adventurous diver can frequently see less restored and considerably wetter and blurrier artifacts. A wreck that is not present but that has left its contemporary and eternal mark is that of the *Wellwood*, a 400-foot Turkish freighter which ran aground within the park's boundaries in the fall of 1984. The *Wellwood*, filled with chicken feed, and captained, it would certainly seem, with some incompetence by a C. H. Vickers, ignored the 45-foot flashing light that marks Molasses Reef on the southernmost boundary of the park and ploughed into the reef, annihilating four acres of living coral. It made a portion of that fabulous tract, all the peaks and valleys and colorful caves bright with life, as flat and as gray as a parking lot.

The reef that runs along the Atlantic coast of the Keys, close to the great Gulf Stream, is fantastically fragile. All reefs are complex and highly particular life-forms, requiring lots of sunlight and clear, warm water. The Florida Keys tract (the only reef in the continental United States) exists at the northernmost limit

CORAL REEF
Smallmouth grunts school in the shadows of elkhorn coral in the reefs off Key Largo. (Photograph © Doug Perrine/Innerspace Visions)

of tropical reef development. It is threatened by this potentially chilly location. It is threatened by its own wonderful accessibility. It is threatened by development on land, by boat bilge, by silt dredged up from marinas, by the effluent and rainwater runoff from condo complexes and parking lots. It is threatened by overuse and misuse. With all this close at hand, it seems cruel and unnecessary for fate to bring tons of chicken feed blundering out of the darkness for the singular purpose of extinguishing part of beautiful Molasses Reef, but blunder out of the darkness the chicken feed did. (More recently, a 147-foot freighter carrying candy and cigarettes deliberately grounded on Western Sambo Reef in the Lower Keys during a winter storm, demolishing that.) The Park Service has marked off the damaged tract with yellow cone-shaped buoys and are monitoring it for signs of regeneration, which they do not expect to occur. The part of the reef visited by the wayward *Wellwood* has ceased to exist. It has become part of Keys history, as gone as the Caloosa Indians, the railroad, and the green turtle.

≈

Wallace Stevens wrote *her mind had bound me round*—and he was speaking of Key West. This peculiar and unlikely town does have a mind quite of her own, with attitudes and habits that can either charm or exasperate, seduce or dismay the new acquaintance. The traveler seldom wants to see what he sees, he wants to see something else. And in many respects, Key West, which is so singular in its architecture and attitude, its posturing and fancifulness, its zany eclecticism, its seedy tropicality, is a town come upon unseen, unexpected, the something else almost felt. It is an urbane, isolated, freewheeling, lighthearted, gossipy, and eccentric town. There is a sense of adventure here, of excess and individuality. It's odd. Actually odd. It is a rather dirty town and has very little dignity, but it has style. Its architecture is a charming, intriguing mélange of fine houses and shacks, painted primly white or weathered right down to the silvery bone, a mix of gingerbread grandeur and mañana collapse with an abundance of verandas and porticos, columns and pilasters and balconies. Comparison and exception are everywhere. The town can look somewhat like old New England, but with a decidedly un-puritanical cast. Jonathan Edwards would never have slept here. The Navy is a presence, certainly, owning a good quarter of the town as well as two thirds of the waterfront and

all of Boca Chica, but it is not a highly visible one from land. From the air and water the extent of its holdings is clearly seen—the piers and berths, the housing, the ammunition dumps, the runways, the radar towers. In the early 1980's, when the military was, to a considerable extent, pulling out of Key West, the former mayor water-skied to Cuba in an attempt to get the Navy to stay in full force by demonstrating how close that island was to our shores. The mayor water-skied to Cuba. It took him six hours and ten minutes. Key West, being Key West, didn't even think it a particularly strange thing to do.

Homosexuals, who probably command another quarter of the town in terms of real estate and influence, are more visible, providing a sleek and somewhat mordant glaze to the town. Tennessee Williams came to Key West in the 1940's, attracted by the sailors, who all seemed "to be walking to the tune of Managua, Nicaragua," and was influential in introducing the town to artistic gays. Now, many of the shops, guest houses, and dance halls are owned by gays, and much of the town's restoration is attributable to them.

Key West is tolerant, very tolerant. What passes for the society column in the local paper, the *Citizen*, abounds in news of gay couples and events, and a wooden pier that elbowed out into the Atlantic and was a popular lounging spot for years before it collapsed (now recrudescent) was known breezily as "Dick Dock." Gays provide much of the gloss, sophistication, and outrageousness of Key West, as well as the money which keeps the town bubbling along.

Key West is tropical. Island. Cuban. Black. In the morning one hears roosters crowing, although the sense is not particularly bucolic. Some are fighting cocks bred for the gambling pit. The birds pecking in dusty runs beneath towering breadfruit trees are a good example of the decadence and innocence that is Key West. As is the sight of a charred and blackened lot where once a fine old building stood—a lot that might remain charred and empty for years, accepting with the seasons the bougainvillea petals that fall upon the smashed bottles there.

One knows where Key West lies in a geographic sense. Forty-five miles north of the Tropic of Cancer. Closer to Cuba at 90 miles than it is to Miami at almost 150. Due south of Cleveland, Ohio. (Cleveland, Ohio!) A glittering, balmy, perhaps not terribly legitimate rock beneath vast sea skies. Key West's economy over the years has been based on a curious and volatile array of occupations—wrecking, shrimping, fishing, and smuggling. In the 1970's, certainly most of the money that came into Key West was drug money, but things have quieted down somewhat in that regard. Now the money comes from real estate. And things are changing fast.

Key West is now a tourist town—one million people visit it each year—but it is still a town of contrast and contradiction, threat and carelessness and charm. The bars should be sampled, of course, and the reef investigated. The gold should be seen, and the forts and the galleries. One should dance or stand on one of the balconies that line Duval and watch the prowl of the street. The beaches should be duly attended and a tan obtained. The yellowtail stuffed with crabmeat should be eaten, and conch fritters and, since you must, Key lime pie. Café con leche or the intense little energizing espresso called *bucce* must be bought from the window of a Cuban grocery. The flowers and trees should be puzzled over and appreciated, and their lovely names said aloud. Jacaranda. Bougainvillea. Poinciana. Frangipani. One should catch a fish. One should be in the water, and travel over and on the water as much as possible. And, when one is on land, one must assuredly walk. Stroll, linger, wander. For Key West is a walking town, and a bicycling one too. Architectural surprises are around every corner, and other interesting sights less classifiable.

BIG CATCH
Sport fishing off the Florida coasts drew anglers from around the globe. Many were lured by visions of big catches as described in the written exploits of Ernest Hemingway, center, and other authors such as Zane Grey.

A
full big
glass of
FLORIDA
ORANGE
JUICE

For the Vitamin C you need every day!

...one vitamin your body can't store up

The higher the sun goes, the better that big frosty glass of Florida orange juice tastes! It *really* cools you— *scientists say it actually lowers your body temperature.* And a full big glass gives you the vitamin C you need for pep and energy—the "C" you need *every day* because your body can't store it up.

So isn't it lucky that Florida stores its "C"-rich orange juice in cans, all squeezed for you! Keep some icy cold in your refrigerator.

Florida Canned

Ready to serve at a moment's notice. Natural full strength with vitamin and nutritional values. You'll enjoy blended Florida Orange-Grapefruit juice in cans, too.

Florida Fresh-Frozen Concentrate

Tree-fresh flavor with vitamin and nutritional values—in new handy form. P.. juice. *No sugar added.* Keep in freezing compartment. To serve, add three parts water, shake or stir, pour full big glass.

Florida Oranges

Florida Citrus Commission, Lakeland, Florida

Oranges

By John McPhee

John McPhee has become famous for his reporting and nonfiction writing. As a young man, he dreamed of writing for the *New Yorker* and focused his career on joining the staff. After years as a television scriptwriter and *Time* magazine reporter—and after collecting fourteen years worth of rejection slips from the *New Yorker* and other journals—he succeeded.

McPhee honed his craft as a staff writer for the *New Yorker* during the magazine's heyday. Soon, he began to use his talents for literary nonfiction to write books, penning some two dozen titles to date on everything from birchbark canoes to the titanic struggle between man and nature. Among his best known works are *Coming Into the Country* (1977) about the Alaskan wilderness and the people who live there; and *Basin and Range* (1981), explaining the geology of America. In 1999, McPhee won the Pulitzer Prize for Nonfiction for his book *Annals of the Former World* (1998).

Oranges, first published in 1966, examines the history of the common fruit and the world of the orange growers. This excerpt is an apt introduction to oranges and the beauty of McPhee's prose.

"A FULL BIG GLASS OF FLORIDA ORANGE JUICE"
This 1960s advertisement touted Florida's "liquid sunshine," which was bottled for thirsty orange-juice lovers everywhere.

THE FIRST KNOWN reference to oranges occurs in the second book of the *Five Classics,* which appeared in China around 500 B.C. and is generally regarded as having been edited by Confucius. The main course of the migration of the fruit—from its origins near the South China Sea, down into the Malay Archipelago, then on four thousand miles of ocean current to the east coast of Africa, across the desert by caravan and into the Mediterranean basin, then over the Atlantic to the American continents—closely and sometimes exactly kept pace with the major journeys of civilization. There were no oranges in the Western Hemisphere before Columbus himself introduced them. It was Pizarro who took them to Peru. The seeds the Spaniards carried came from trees that had entered Spain as a result of the rise of Islam. The development of orange botany owes something to Vasco da Gama and even more to Alexander the Great; oranges had symbolic importance in the paintings of Renaissance masters; in other times, at least two overwhelming invasions of the Italian peninsula were inspired by the visions of paradise that oranges engendered in northern minds. Oranges were once the fruit of the gods, to whom they were the golden apples of the Hesperides, which were stolen by Hercules. Then, in successive declensions, oranges became the fruit of emperors and kings, of the upper prelacy, of the aristocracy, and, by the eighteenth century, of the rich bourgeoisie. Another hundred years went by before they came within reach of the middle classes, and not until early in this century did they at last become a fruit of the community.

Just after the Second World War, three scientists working in central Florida surprised themselves with a simple idea that resulted in the development of commercial orange-juice concentrate. A couple of dozen enormous factories sprang out of the hammocks, and Florida, which can be counted on in most seasons to produce about a quarter of all the oranges grown in the world, was soon putting most of them through the process that results in small, trim cans, about two inches in diameter and four inches high, containing orange juice that has been boiled to high viscosity in a vacuum, separated into several component parts, reassembled, flavored, and then frozen solid. People in the United States used to consume more fresh oranges than all other fresh fruits combined, but in less than twenty years the per-capita consumption has gone

down seventy-five per cent, as appearances of actual oranges in most of the United States have become steadily less frequent. Fresh, whole, round, orange oranges are hardly extinct, of course, but they have seen better days since they left the garden of the Hesperides.

Fresh oranges have become, in a way, old-fashioned. The frozen product made from them is pure and sweet, with a laboratory-controlled balance between its acids and its sugars; its color and its flavor components are as uniform as science can make them, and a consumer opening the six-ounce can is confident that the drink he is about to reconstitute will taste almost exactly like the juice that he took out of the last can he bought. Fresh orange juice, on the other hand, is probably less consistent in flavor than any other natural or fermented drink, with the possible exception of wine.

The taste and aroma of oranges differ by type, season, county, state, and country, and even as a result of the position of the individual orange in the framework of the tree on which it grew. Ground fruit—the orange that one can reach and pick from the ground—is not as sweet as fruit that grows high on the tree. Outside fruit is sweeter than inside fruit. Oranges grown on the south side of a tree are sweeter than oranges grown on the east or west sides, and oranges grown on the north side are the least sweet of the lot. The quantity of juice in an orange, and even the amount of Vitamin C it contains, will follow the same pattern of variation. Beyond this, there are differentiations of quality inside a single orange. Individual segments vary from one another in their content of acid and sugar. But that is cutting it pretty fine. Orange men, the ones who actually work in the groves, don't discriminate to that extent. When they eat an orange, they snap out the long, thin blades of their fruit knives and peel it down, halfway, from the blossom end, which is always sweeter and juicier than the stem end. They eat the blossom half and throw the rest of the orange away.

An orange grown in Florida usually has a thin and tightly fitting skin, and it is also heavy with juice. Californians say that if you want to eat a Florida orange you have to get into a bathtub first. California oranges are light in weight and have thick skins that break easily and come off in hunks. The flesh inside is marvelously sweet, and the segments almost separate themselves. In Florida, it is said that you can run over a

Picking Oranges near Ft. Myers

ORANGE GROVES
*Workers pick oranges near Fort Myers in this postcard scene
from the 1930s.*

enough to change the color; in Thailand, for example, an orange is a green fruit, and traveling Thais often blink with wonder at the sight of oranges the color of flame. The ideal nighttime temperature in an orange grove is forty degrees. Some of the most beautiful oranges in the world are grown in Bermuda, where the temperature, night after night, falls consistently to that level. Andrew Marvell's poem wherein the "remote Bermudas ride in the ocean's bosom unespied" was written in the sixteen-fifties, and contains a description, from hearsay, of Bermuda's remarkable oranges, set against their dark foliage like "golden lamps in a green night."

Cool air comes down every night into the San Joaquin Valley in California, which is formed by the Coast Range to the west and the Sierra Nevadas to the east. The tops of the Sierras are usually covered with snow, and before dawn the temperature in the valley edges down to the frost point. In such cosmetic surroundings, it is no wonder that growers have heavily implanted the San Joaquin Valley with the Washington Navel Orange, which is the most beautiful orange grown in any quantity in the United States, and is certainly as attractive to the eye as any orange grown in the world. Its color will go to a deep, flaring cadmium orange, and its surface has a suggestion of coarseness, which complements its perfect ellipsoid shape.

Among orange groups, the navel orange is an old one. In his *Hesperides, or Four Books on the Culture and Use of the Golden Apples*, Giovanni Battista Ferrari, a Sienese Jesuit priest of the seventeenth century, described it, saying: "This orange imitates to some extent the fertility of the tree which bears it, in that it struggles, though unsuccessfully, to reproduce the fruit upon itself." It is thus a kind of monster. Just beneath the navel-like opening in the blossom end of each navel orange, there is a small and, more or less, fetal orange, usually having five or six pithy segments. The navel strain that we know now originated in Bahia, Brazil, probably as a bud sport, or mutation, of the Brazilian Selecta Orange. In 1870, an American Presbyterian missionary in Bahia was impressed by the seedlessness and rich flavor of this unusual orange with an umbilicus at its blossom end, and sent twelve

California orange with a ten-ton truck and not even wet the pavement. The differences from which these hyperboles arise will prevail in the two states even if the type of orange is the same. In arid climates, like California's, oranges develop a thick albedo, which is the white part of the skin. Florida is one of the two or three most rained-upon states in the United States. California uses the Colorado River and similarly impressive sources to irrigate its oranges, but of course irrigation can only do so much. The annual difference in rainfall between the Florida and California orange-growing areas is one million one hundred and forty thousand gallons per acre. For years, California was the leading orange state, but Florida surpassed California in 1942, and grows three times as many oranges now. California oranges, for their part, can safely be called three times as beautiful.

The color of an orange has no absolute correlation with the maturity of the flesh and juice inside. An orange can be as sweet and ripe as it will ever be and still glisten like an emerald in the tree. Cold—coolness, rather—is what makes an orange orange. In some parts of the world, the weather never gets cold

CLASSIC CITRUS CRATE ARTWORK
The glories of Florida's orange and grapefruit crops were hailed in the artwork on these 1930s crate labels.

nursery-size trees to the United States Department of Agriculture in Washington. The department propagated the trees and sent the progeny to anyone who cared to give them a try. In 1873, Mrs. Luther C. Tibbets, of Riverside, California, wrote for a pair of trees, got them, and planted them in her yard. Mrs. Tibbets' trees caught the attention of her neighbors and, eventually, of the world. From them have descended virtually every navel orange grown anywhere on earth today, including the Carter, the Golden Nugget, the Surprise, the Golden Buckeye, the Robertson, and the Thomson. The patriarchal one should by rights be called the Bahia, but merely because of its brief residence in the District of Columbia it has been known for ninety-six years as the Washington Navel Orange.

In the United States, in a typical year, around twenty-five billion oranges are grown. These include, among others, Maltese Ovals, Pope Summers, Nonpareils, Rubys, Sanford Bloods, Early Oblongs, Magnum Bonums, St. Michaels, Mediterranean Sweets, Lamb Summers, Lue Gim Gongs, Drake Stars, Whites, Whittakers, Weldons, Starks, Osceolas, Majorcas, Homosassas, Enterprises, Arcadias, Circassians, Centennials, Fosters, Dillars, Bessies, and Boones, but not—in all of these cases—in any appreciable quantity. Actually, one variety alone constitutes fully half of the total crop. Originally known in California as the Rivers Late Orange and in Florida as the Hart's Tardiff, it was imported into the United States early in the eighteen-seventies in unlabeled packages from the Thomas Rivers Nursery, of Sawbridgeworth, Hertfordshire. The easygoing Mr. Rivers had not only left off the name of the orange trees; he also failed to note where he had found them. They grew to be big, vigorous trees that bore remarkable quantities of almost seedless fruit containing lots of juice, which had a racy tartness in delicious proportion to its ample sugars. As supposedly different varieties, the trees were already beginning to prosper when an orange grower from Spain, traveling in California, felt suddenly at home in a grove of the so-called Rivers Lates. "That," said the Spanish grower, clearing up all mysteries with one unequivocal remark, "is the Late Orange of Valencia."

Out of the bewildering catalogue of orange varieties and strains, the Valencia has emerged in this century as something close to a universal orange. It is more widely and extensively planted than any other. From Florida and California and Central and South America to South Africa and Australia, Valencias grow in abundance in nearly all the orange centers of the world except Valencia. Having given the world the most remunerative orange yet known, Spain now specializes in its celebrated strains of bloods and navels. Only two per cent of the Spanish crop are Valencias, and perhaps only half of that comes from the groves of Valencia itself; much of the remainder grows in old, untended groves near Seville, where cattle wander through and munch oranges on the trees, on either bank of the Guadalquivir.

The Valencia is a spring and summer orange, and the Washington Navel ripens in the fall and winter. The two varieties overlap twice with perfect timing in California—where together, they are almost all of the total crop—and the orange industry there never stops. In Florida, the Valencia harvest begins in late March and ends in June, and for about four months there is no picking. Florida grows few navel oranges, somewhat to the state's embarrassment. Florida growers tried hard enough, some seventy or eighty years ago, but the Washington Navel, in the language of pomology, proved to be too shy a bearer there. Instead, to meet the fall and winter markets, Florida growers have a number of locally developed early varieties to choose from, and in the main they seem to prefer three: the Pineapple Orange, the Parson Brown, and the Hamlin.

The Pineapple developed in the eighteen-seventies and was so named because its full, heavy aroma gave packinghouse employees the feeling that they were working in Hawaii rather than in Florida. The Pineapple is fairly seedy, usually containing about a dozen seeds, but it is rich in flavor, loaded with juice, and pretty to look at, with its smooth-textured, bright-orange skin and its slightly elongated shape. The skin is weak, though, and highly subject to decay. Most oranges, with appropriate care, will live about a month after they are picked. Pineapple Oranges don't have anything like that kind of stamina. (The Temple Orange and the Murcott Honey Orange, which are not actually oranges, ripen at the same time that Pineapples do. They are natural hybrids, almost certainly tangors—half orange, half tangerine—and they are so sweet that people on diets sometimes eat them before dinner in order to throttle their appetites. Oranges float, but these have so much sugar in them that if you drop one into a bucket of water it will go straight to the bottom. Murcotts were named for Charles Murcott Smith, one of the first men to propagate them. Advertisements have, from time to time, claimed that Temple Oranges were native to the Orient and sacred to a little-known sect of the Buddhist faith, and the seeds from which Florida's trees eventually sprang were stolen from a temple against the resistance of guardian priests. Temple Oranges are in fact named for William Chase Temple, who, long ago, was general manager of the Florida Citrus Exchange.)

Parson Nathan L. Brown was a Florida clergyman who grew oranges to supplement his income; the seedy, pebble-skinned orange that now carries his name was discovered in his grove about a hundred years ago. It tends to have pale-yellow flesh and pale-yellow juice, for, in general, the color of orange juice is light among early-season oranges, deeper in mid-season varieties, and deeper still in late ones.

The seedless, smooth-skinned Hamlin, also named for a Florida grove owner, ripens in October, ordinarily about two weeks ahead of the Parson Brown.

Both Hamlins and Parson Browns, when they are harvested, are usually as green as grass. They have to be ripe, because an orange will not continue to ripen after it has been picked. Many other fruits—apples and pears, for example—go on ripening for weeks after they leave the tree. Their flesh contains a great deal of starch, and as they go on breathing (all fruit breathes until it dies, and should be eaten before it is dead), they gradually convert the starch to sugar. When oranges breathe, there is no starch within them to be converted. Whatever sugars, acids, and flavor essences they have were necessarily acquired on the tree. Hence, an advertisement for "tree-ripened" oranges is essentially a canard. There is no other way to ripen oranges. It is against the law to market oranges that are not tree-ripened—that is to say, oranges that are not ripe. Women see a patch or even a hint of green on an orange in a store and they seem to feel that they are making a knowledgeable decision when they avoid it. Some take home a can of concentrated orange juice instead. A good part, if not all, of the juice inside the can may have come from perfectly ripe, bright-green oranges.

Some oranges that become orange while they are still unripe may turn green again as they ripen. When cool nights finally come to Florida, around the first of the year, the Valencia crop is fully developed in size and shape, but it is still three months away from ripeness. Sliced through the middle at that time, a Valencia looks something like a partitioned cupful of rice, and its taste is overpoweringly acid. But in the winter coolness, the exterior surface turns to bright orange, and the Valencia appears to be perfect for picking. Warm nights return, however, during the time of the Valencia harvest. On the trees in late spring, the Valencias turn green again, growing sweeter each day and greener each night.

CHAPTER 2

Old Florida

"Outside it was a lovely, cool, sub-tropical winter day and the palm branches were sawing in the light north wind. Some winter people rode by the house on bicycles. They were laughing. In the big yard of the house across the street a peacock squawked. Through the window you could see the sea looking hard and new and blue in the winter light."
—Ernest Hemingway, writing of Key West in To Have and Have Not, *1937*

History moves quickly in a place such as Florida. The old is razed as the new is erected, the population swells daily, and the natural world shrinks. The spirit of old Florida lives on, however, in the art and writing as well as the stories and tall tales handed down to subsequent generations.

***Above:* Ybor City Cigarmaker**
Beginning in the 1880s, Cuban immigrants found work in the bustling cigar factories of old Ybor City in Tampa. As shown in this photograph from the 1910s, cigars were fashioned by hand, just as they had been in Havana, Cuba. (Florida State Archives Photographic Collection)

***Opposite Page:* Fort Castillo de San Marcos**
Fort Castillo de San Marcos guarded the old Spanish city of St. Augustine, the first permanent European settlement on the continent. The city was founded in 1565, forty-two years before the settlement at Jamestown, Virginia, and fifty-five years before the pilgrims landed at Plymouth Rock. Built between 1672 and 1695, the fort ruled over St. Augustine's bay and protected the sea route for Spanish galleons returning to Spain with their New World treasures. (Photograph © Eric Dusenbery/Dimensions Photography)

The Tropic of Cracker

By Al Burt

Al Burt has a broad sense of humor, especially when it comes to his native state of Florida. His books, columns, and articles reveal a writer who is equal parts folklorist, reporter, and storyteller.

Burt was a roving columnist for the *Miami Herald* for twenty-two years, a job that gave him license to interview and write about the heroes of ordinary life in the Sunshine State. Along with some four decades of journalism work and numerous magazine articles, he has published several books, including *Florida: A Place in the Sun* (1974), *Becalmed in the Mullet Latitudes* (1983), and *Al Burt's Florida: Snowbirds, Sand Castles, and Self-Rising Crackers* (1997).

This excerpt from his book *The Tropic of Cracker* (1999) displays Burt's sense of humor, his writing abilities, and his drive to preserve the history of his beloved Florida.

CRACKER CRABBER
A commercial crabber rests after a hard day's work and a good haul of crabs on Horseshoe Beach in the Panhandle. (Photograph © Tony Arruza)

CRACKER COWBOYS

Florida is cattle country. The state boasts a history of ranching that dates back to the days of statehood. Here, Cracker cowboys drive cattle on Three Rivers Ranch in Zephyrhills. As Florida author Ernest Lyons noted in his essay "A Florida Cracker Comes Into His Own": "A Cracker may rise to be a supreme court justice or a governor, but his heart stays at the ranch with his cows, catch-dogs and rattlesnakes." (Photograph © Maresa Pryor)

IN THE TROPIC of Cracker there are no parallels staked out, circling the earth at certain degrees and so many minutes above the equator, marking a zone and rendering scholarly identification of the climate and range of life. The Tropic of Cracker has no boundaries. In Florida it simply occurs, as unbidden as sandspurs or wildflowers, rooting in the minds of Floridians who have links to their past and kinship to their native heritage. Without forgetting practicality, it lifts spirits and fires imaginations.

Sometimes discomforting things invoke the Tropic of Cracker—bugs and weeds and thunderstorms and heat and humidity—and sometimes it wafts in on the stimulation of things more majestic. It can arrive, for example, with one of those Florida sunsets so awesome that if they happened in just one place and at just one time each year, rather than all over the state every evening, they would be tourist attractions all by themselves. If there were only one annual Florida sunset it would be worth traveling hundreds of miles to see, as are the brilliant changes of leaf color each fall

in the Blue Ridge Mountains.

Wildflowers splashing a simple trail of color across a drab field can induce it. Individual sensitivities determine it. Whatever brings to the mind a confirming identification with native Florida, whatever reassures that there can be natural beauty and treasured culture among common folk and in common places can conjure up the Tropic of Cracker.

It has no created facade. It was not invented to please a stranger for the purpose of taking his money, though that might be a side benefit. It simply celebrates native Florida, the full scope of it, the free-flowing rivers and the beautifully framing beaches and the clear springs, the mythic swamps where only the sound of the wind or the cry of an animal breaks the silence, the great stretches of forests where night falls black without the interruption of halogen lamps. It revels in the sights and songs of untamed things, the yodel and gobble of sandhill cranes cruising the prairies and pastures, the bobwhite call of a quail or the mourning coo of a dove, pelicans squawking on a Keys dock or gulls lobbying fishing boats for a handout, exuberant mullet jumping clear in the bays, pursued shrimp skittering across the surface of inlets, buzzards poetically circling over a downtown courthouse.

From nurtured backyard jungles to the great vistas of the Everglades, from the magical Keys to the thousands of clear lakes socketed into central Florida sandhills, from river-sweetened estuaries to dune-guarded beaches where Spanish conquistadores once splashed ashore, the Tropic of Cracker represents what remains of the Florida that needed no blueprint or balance sheet for its creation, that was here before there was a can opener or a commercial or a real-estate agent.

Crackers inhabit the Tropic of Cracker, and they are called that either because they are natives of Florida or because they so love the native things of Florida that they have been naturalized by experience and exposure. People argue about the use of the word "Cracker," but it does not matter. In Florida, the word comes out of state history. Old-time cow hunters drove great herds of cattle across Florida to shipping points, popping long cowhide whips so loudly that they could be heard miles ahead. Because of this, they became known as Crackers. The Florida definition has nothing to do with race. It is a tribal feather, not a street slur. Some Snowbirds, some newcomers who arrive wanting to teach Florida lessons rather than to learn the lessons of Florida, have trouble with that. Let them learn. They probably did not understand about aquifers or sinkholes or kumquats or gopher tortoises when they arrived, either. They have a treat in store. We are willing to share.

Crackers come in all sizes and shapes and backgrounds and beliefs. As Florida leapfrogged from a frontier to a megastate on wave after wave of migration, backwoods Crackers whose families had seeped down across the borders from Alabama or Georgia chasing one of the booms dwindled from dominance, but not from influence. . . .

In the quarter century after World War II, when migration at its peak brought in a net gain of 1,000 new Floridians per day, a new kind of urban or suburban Cracker began to emerge. These typically were the old Crackers with the rough edges buffed off, or the sons and daughters and grandchildren of those old Crackers, far enough removed that they could look back on the hard times of the earlier years and see them as quaint, or even romantic. Attitudes changed,

SPONGE MARKET
Harvesting sponges was big business in Florida for decades until the advent of synthetic sponges in the 1940s. Key West was the center of the sponge trade until the sponge beds were over-harvested. Sponge fishermen then moved on to Tarpon Springs and other more fertile beds. Here, buyers examine the sponge harvest in 1895 at the Apalachicola sponge market along the old wharves. (Florida State Archives Photographic Collection)

SPONGE DIVER
The city of Tarpon Springs blossomed with the arrival of Greek sponge fisherman John Corcoris. With the aid of old-fashioned copper diving helmets and deep-sea suits, Corcoris and his Greek divers descended into deep-water sponge beds and harvested the aquatic animals. The sponge industry in Tarpon Springs grew into a multi-million-dollar venture.

SPONGE FISHERMAN FLEET
Greek sponge-fishing boats arrive in the harbor at Key West with a full harvest of sponges drying on lines.

SUNRISE OVER CEDAR KEYS

The sun rises over oyster beds in the Cedar Keys. Just a century ago, the city of Cedar Key was the largest in the state, centered around a bustling port and a pencil-manufacturing industry that crafted writing utensils from cedarwood. Cedar Key never regained its former stature following a hurricane in 1896, but it is world famous today among seafood lovers for its restaurants and Seafood Festival. (Photograph © Maresa Pryor)

growth that changed the landscape and wiped out familiar vistas and landmarks. They were chagrined to see the Florida landscape being crimped and bent to give it an ambience imported from some other place. Many of them became absorbed with saving the Florida they knew, with the ideal of a Florida that honored its own nature. These were citizens who clung to the hope that growth need not necessarily mean the trashing of a great state. For them, the Tropic of Cracker had the aura of truth.

The old Crackers did not fade without significant grumbling about the changes. Some of them just hated to give up their mules for tractors, and didn't. Others dwelled on a change in values and attitudes. . . . Changes wrought by Florida migration were daunting for almost all, even the reasonable. Throughout Florida history, wave after wave of newcomers invaded. One wave after the Civil War moved Florida's population from 140,000 in 1860 to 270,000 in 1880 (about 65 percent native born). Other waves came along during the 1920s boom, jumping the population to 928,000 in 1920 and to 1.5 million by 1930, during the Depression. In a post-World War II surge, the leaps became even larger, more than tripling in the next three decades to some 9 million in 1980 (up 564 percent since 1930), adding another 3 million in the 1980s (about two-thirds born somewhere else). As the year 2000 approached, Floridians numbered some 14 million plus 40 million or so tourists each year.

So the story of Florida in large part became a story of numbers, of the many from somewhere else who were so attracted to the extraordinary Florida nature that they stampeded here with their different notions of lifestyle, many wanting to mark it with their initials, to brand it with their own customs, to taste it and feel it and digest it and reshape it into all sorts of forms that had been favored in those other places where they had lived.

In a state like this, the Crackers began to understand, intelligent analysis could be made only if it were judged against itself, by its own standards and by its own natural treasures—not by the standards of some other place with far worse problems and a different history of how and why it arrived to them. It became a Cracker axiom that Florida couldn't truly measure its loss and gain and potential except by comparison with the good and bad of what life had been like here in Florida. Without remembering how it was, we could not know how it could be. Without remembering how

interests diversified, horizons broadened. Like almost everybody else in America, the Crackers too grew up.

Appreciative natives—folklife historians, environmentalists, naturalists and their kin, simple defenders of the feel and flavors of an old Florida lifestyle, but not of the narrower social outlook—became the new Crackers. They were simply proud Floridians, housebroken and optimistic, perturbed by swamping new

FLORIDA PLANTATION
The opulence of bygone days and a way of life now remote remain at Wesley Mansion and Eden State Gardens near Point Washington. Built in the late 1800s by a lumber baron, the stately, white-columned mansion was crafted of local cypress and heart-pine wood. (Photograph © Eric Dusenbery/Dimensions Photography)

FORT PICKENS

Pensacola was settled by Spanish explorers in 1559, six years before St. Augustine, but was abandoned due to Indian attacks and hurricanes. Across the bay from the city on Santa Rosa Island, Fort Pickens did battle with the mainland's Fort Barrancas during the Civil War—in fact, some historians believe the first shots of the conflict were fired here rather than at Fort Sumter. Today, Fort Pickens maintains a lonely watch over the island's sand dunes. (Photograph © Eric Dusenbery/Dimensions Photography)

it was, we could not know whether the new diversity, the new conveniences, the broadened horizons were worth what had been sacrificed for them. In some cases, they began to feel, the new job opportunities and the enlarged economy and the heightened awareness of the world took place at considerable cost. Florida began to lose some of its distinguishing peculiarities. Beaches grew crowded, traffic became congested, extraordinary natural vistas fell before bulldozers, the air and water began to suffer pollution, marine life was damaged, wading birds decreased, crime and stress went up, and the suicide and divorce rates shot up per capita among the leaders in the nation.

To preserve some sense of natural Florida and a lifestyle geared to it, there needed to be some spiritual first aid for the Cracker soul. One place it came from was such inventions as the Tropic of Cracker, paying homage to custom and mood and preference. It was like a pledge of allegiance, or maybe a prayer, for Florida.

Cracker faithful believed it was essential that Floridians keep in mind the special dimensions of Florida. They thought Floridians needed to understand this place if they were to live here and make reasonable decisions about it. They needed to understand that a sense of Florida depended upon assimilating all its brilliant points and counterpoints. They needed to remember that although a sandy spine anchors the middle of this peninsula that separates the Atlantic and the Gulf, almost everything that affects the interior makes its way to the water and affects the coast, and almost everything affecting the coast also impacts the interior.

Floridians needed to remember that as this state rises out of the beautiful subtropics and climbs into the temperate zone, immense change unfolds. Not only the weather and the temperatures change: The geography goes from sea level to hilly, the terrain from desertlike to swampy, the soil from sugar sands to muck and red clay. Each of those variations represents the preferences of living things, certain people and certain plants and certain animals, and each of those cluster to the parts they prefer. Within all that, almost everything moves and shifts and circles and returns in patterns—migrating human populations, ocean tides, birds and marine life. Florida thrives on mobility and change, and these affect all living things. In Florida, there are differences enough for all to find their special place.

If the Tropic of Cracker could be made real, by a Cracker Disney, all the houses would have front porches on which sat rockers. Every evening the family would sit there and wave to neighbors taking a walk. Everybody would smile a lot, because Crackers think a smile defines the breadth of the human dimension. They would try to charm the whole world, one yard at a time. . . .

All those things are part of the collective Cracker memory and heritage. The Tropic of Cracker recalls a sense of it all—the landscape of old Florida and what there remains of it, quaintly tacky in many of its man-made aspects, natively ragged in nearly all ways, but still so purely beautiful it could inspire even a tourist to pray that this should last forever. It is not tourist Florida, not I-75 or I-95 or high-rise Florida, not the TV-ad Florida behind tinted glass with soft lights and cool temperatures even in August, not the billboard Florida that issues maps locating the attractions with cute cartoon figures.

The Tropic of Cracker, in all its imaginary grandeur, is a matter of plain folk and an unashamed tethering to the land, an affection as pure as puppy dog love, love of Grandma and Grandpa, or love of a new baby in an old family. It is a thing of the mind, a matter of memories and appreciations, of recalling people and things and places that you would sacrifice to bring back, things whose value goes beyond the measure of numbers.

For some, the smell of an orange blossom triggers it. For others, the sight of Spanish moss hanging off the twisted black limbs of a live oak. For a few, reminders of the wild bring it alive—the roar of a bull gator, or maybe the leap of a dolphin between a swimmer and the shore, or a rattlesnake defensively coiling under a palmetto and flicking its forked tongue and angrily rattling its tail. The oddly sweetish taste of a fresh muscadine grape might do it, or the shock of a dive into the exhilaratingly cold waters of a deep spring where thousands of bubbles trail across the body and curious fish swim close to see the intruder. The sound of the first chuck-will's-widow in the spring could induce it, or the sight of lightning bugs bumping against the windows at night, flashing semaphore signals from the wild.

A tall white egret elegantly stalking the lakeshore, readying the spear of its beak for a quick snap at a live snack, calls it up; beach dunes rippled and silkened by the wind; those old rust-streaked oranges that scientists later made perfectly orange to please the Snowbirds; the distinctly wry and character-building taste of grapefruit that a Cracker could imagine eating up the cholesterol and strengthening the principles, but now sweet and tinted, like soda pop.

The Tropic of Cracker feeds a bit on nostalgia, sure, but there is more to it than that. There is the aspect of trying to defend home and trying to inspire others to help, of wanting to shuck off past evils and celebrate the good things of old Florida. It is the feeling that here there has been something special that should not be lost or forgotten, something not just confined to the library or to a museum or to a vault. There is a desire to cull the best of heritage and weave it back into daily life.

The Tropic of Cracker requires imagination, but it represents commitments blooded and boned into the lives of Floridians as they grew up. Those feelings become the idealized vision of home. Nothing can change them.

The BRIAR BOWL
MIAMI BEACH
CIGARS
CIGARETTES
FILMS HERE
CIGARETTES
MIXTURE
69
OPTIMO
BAR

Cigars

By José Yglesias

José Yglesias wrote fourteen books, many of which evoked and paid homage to the world of the cigar-makers of Ybor City, the old Cuban and Italian section of Tampa where he grew up and lived most of his life.

Yglesias was one of the pioneering Latino writers in the United States and is considered by many as a father of Latino fiction. He published numerous novels, essays, magazine articles, and memoirs, including *The Goodbye Land* (1967), *In the Fist of the Revolution: Life in a Cuban Country Town* (1968), and *The Truth About Them* (1971).

This excerpt from Yglesias's first novel, *A Wake in Ybor City* (1963), is a small jewel of writing. In this passage he outlines the intersection between the old and the new, traditional Cuban life in Tampa and the changes Cuban-American society faced in the name of progress.

FELIZ SMILED CAUTIOUSLY. He took two cigars from his breast pocket and held one out to Jaime. "Would you like one?"

Jaime took the cigar and turned it in his hand, noticing that it had no paper band or cellophane wrapper. "It looks excellent. Is it freshly made?"

Feliz leaned back proudly. "Today fresh from the factory. An old friend of my father brings them to me. They're completely handmade, from the first piece of filler to the leaf wrapper."

Jaime brought it to his face and smelled it carefully. "Havana?'

"Oh yes," Feliz said. "There are still one or two factories that use only Havana tobacco. Not just the wrapper, but the filler, too."

"I see that you know your cigar making," Jaime said politely.

"His father was a foreman at a big factory all his life," Elena said. "He kept the whole family working, thank God."

Jaime turned to Elena and asked, "May I, my dear?"

Elena looked puzzled for a moment. "Of course, of course, you may smoke it in front of us. We are all used to cigar smoke here. It's perfume to us. Isn't that so?" And she turned to Feliz's wife, Teresa.

Teresa was delighted that Elena should ask her. "Oh yes, indeed," she said. "You are so right. It is like perfume to us." She did not look at Feliz because he knew she hated cigar smoke. Feliz had never, however, asked her for permission to light a cigar. Nor would he ever, Teresa thought.

"You're very kind," Jaime said. He hesitated a second and Feliz handed him a wooden match. "Thank you," Jaime said. He neatly punctured the end of the cigar with it.

Feliz did not puncture his cigar with a match. He bit into it and tore a small piece from the end. Then he rolled the end in his mouth, wetting and reforming it. His thick, purplish lips puckered into an O and alternately gripped and let go of the end of the cigar. Having twirled it several times in his mouth, he took it out and looked at it. The end of the cigar was dark with saliva. With his thumbnail he scratched the wooden match until it popped into flame. He put the flame to the cigar first, as if warming it, and still holding the flame at the end of the cigar, he moved the cigar around in his mouth. He twirled it slowly while he puffed and exhaled bluish-gray clouds of smoke.

"Ah!" Feliz said, "in my father's day, the Ybor City factories knew how to make cigars. Alfonso the Thirteenth used to buy Tampa cigars. But the cigar owners didn't know how to advertise, or were too stingy. Instead they began to bring in machines like the American factories use up North. That was the beginning of the end."

Clara went back to examining her nails, buffing them to a high shine. She did not like gatherings where there was no man who belonged to her.

"This is an excellent cigar," Jaime said.

"Because it's made the way a cigar should be made," Feliz explained, and hoped his mother would stay in the kitchen so he could hold the floor. "It's made by one man from beginning to end. No breaking up the process into bunch-makers who take the bunch, put it into a mold, and press it, and rollers who open up the molds and then wrap an artificially cured leaf—

CIGARMAKER'S TOOLS
The tools of the cigarmaker's trade rest on a work table in the Ybor City State Museum. (Photograph © Eric Dusenbery/ Dimensions Photography)

Cigar Making by Spanish Hand Method   Cuesta Rey & Co.

HAND-ROLLING CIGARS
Following unrest in Cuba in the 1880s, many Cubans followed Vincente Martínez Ybor to the promise of a new life in Florida. Ybor set up a cigar factory first in Key West and later in what would become Ybor City in Tampa. Rows of workers meticulously hand-rolled cigars in Ybor's factory while a lectore, *or "reader," read to them from the newspaper or novels of the day. This photograph was taken at the Cuesta-Rey Factory in Tampa in the 1920s. (Florida State Archives Photographic Collection)*

a leaf that has an even green color but no taste around the bunch. No, sir, I won't speak of those machines into which you throw tobacco at one end and even-size brown pieces of rope come out the other! They can't be called cigars. A cigar is an object that a man builds up in his left hand with the help of his right hand that knows how to select and place every piece of long filler—I said *long* filler—into the hollow of that left hand." Feliz held out his left hand, half closed, and moved the fingers over the thumb. "That left hand has to know how to shape the cigar and how much pressure to exert on the tobacco to let the cigar burn evenly later. An honest brown leaf that has been carefully selected should be stretched over it and then it will burn like this." He held up his cigar at an angle. "That ash will hang on to the very end if it's a good cigar."

"Bravo!" said Elena.

"I am convinced," Jaime said. "I'm afraid that feeling the way you do, you must not enjoy working in the new factories."

"Oh me!—never!" Feliz said. "I don't work in the factories. I'm in construction. I build houses. Cigar factories are dying. There's no future in them."

SUNSET IN YBOR CITY
The sun goes down on La Setima *in Ybor City. These streets once throbbed with Cuban immigrant life when Vincente Martínez Ybor's cigar factories were in full swing. Casinos, cafés, cockfights, music, and the speeches of Cuban revolutionaries such as José Martí were all part of the transplanted world. (Photograph © Eric Dusenbery/ Dimensions Photography)*

How it Feels to be Colored Me

By Zora Neale Hurston

Zora Neale Hurston is one of the great figures in twentieth-century American literature and African-American culture. She was a novelist, folklorist, and anthropologist, equal parts a product of the rural black South and the Harlem Renaissance.

Hurston was born in 1890 in the central Florida town of Eatonville, the oldest incorporated black town in the United States. She joined a traveling drama group and then enrolled at Morgan Academy, subsequently studying at Howard University, Barnard College, and Columbia University. Among her most famous works are the folklore collection *Mules and Men* (1935), the novel *Their Eyes Were Watching God* (1937), and her memoir *Dust Tracks on a Road* (1942).

Hurston's essay "How it Feels to be Colored Me" was originally published in the *World Tomorrow* magazine in 1928, and illustrated her rambunctious independence and strong will to overcome all odds.

WREATH OF FLOWERS
A vine heavy with blossoms encircles a rural mailbox in Havana. (Photograph © Tony Arruza)

I AM COLORED but I offer nothing in the way of extenuating circumstances except the fact that I am the only Negro in the United States whose grandfather on the mother's side was *not* an Indian chief.

I remember the very day that I became colored. Up to my thirteenth year I lived in the little Negro town of Eatonville, Florida. It is exclusively a colored town. The only white people I knew passed through the town going to or coming from Orlando. The native whites rode dusty horses, the Northern tourists chugged down the sandy village road in automobiles. The town knew the Southerners and never stopped cane chewing when they passed. But the Northerners were something else again. They were peered at cautiously from behind curtains by the timid. The more venturesome would come out on the porch to watch them go past and got just as much pleasure out of the tourists as the tourists got out of the village.

The front porch might seem a daring place for the rest of the town, but it was a gallery seat to me. My favorite place was atop the gate-post. Proscenium box for a born first-nighter. Not only did I enjoy the show, but I didn't mind the actors knowing that I liked it. I actually spoke to them in passing. I'd wave at them and when they returned my salute, I would say something like this: "Howdy-do-well-I-thank-you-where-you-goin'?" Usually automobile or the horse paused at this, and after a queer exchange of compliments, I would probably "go a piece of the way" with them, as we say in farthest Florida. If one of my family happened to come to the front in time to see me, of course negotiations would be rudely broken off. But even so, it is clear that I was the first "welcome-to-our-state" Floridian, and I hope the Miami Chamber of Commerce will please take notice.

During this period, white people differed from colored to me only in that they rode through town and never lived there. They liked to hear me "speak pieces" and sing and wanted to see me dance the parse-me-la, and gave me generously of their small silver for doing these things, which seemed strange to me for I wanted to do them so much that I needed bribing to stop. Only they didn't know it. The colored people gave no dimes. They deplored any joyful tendencies in me, but I was their Zora nevertheless. I belonged to them, to the nearby hotels, to the county—everybody's Zora.

But changes came in the family when I was thir-teen, and I was sent to school in Jacksonville. I left Eatonville, the town of the oleanders, as Zora. When I disembarked from the riverboat at Jacksonville, she was no more. It seemed that I had suffered a sea change. I was not Zora of Orange County any more, I was now a little colored girl. I found it out in certain ways. In my heart as well as in the mirror, I became a fast brown—warranted not to rub nor run.

But I am not tragically colored. There is no great sorrow dammed up in my soul, nor lurking behind my eyes. I do not mind at all. I do not belong to the sobbing school of Negrohood who hold that nature somehow has given them a lowdown dirty deal and whose feelings are all hurt about it. Even in the helter-skelter skirmish that is my life, I have seen that the world is to the strong regardless of a little pigmentation more or less. No, I do not weep at the world—I am too busy sharpening my oyster knife.

Someone is always at my elbow reminding me that I am the grand-daughter of slaves. It fails to register depression with me. Slavery is sixty years in the past. The operation was successful and the patient is doing well, thank you. The terrible struggle that made me an American out of a potential slave said "On the line!" The Reconstruction said "Get set!"; and the generation before said "Go!" I am off to a flying start and I must not halt in the stretch to look behind and weep. Slavery is the price I paid for civilization, and the choice was not with me. It is a bully adventure and worth all that I have paid through my ancestors for it. No one on earth ever had a greater chance for glory. The world to be won and nothing to be lost. It is thrilling to think—to know that for any act of mine, I shall get twice as much praise or twice as much blame. It is quite exciting to hold the center of the national stage, with the spectators not knowing whether to laugh or to weep.

The position of my white neighbor is much more difficult. No brown specter pulls up a chair beside me when I sit down to eat. No dark ghost thrusts its leg against mine in bed. The game of keeping what one has is never so exciting as the game of getting.

I do not always feel colored. Even now I often achieve the unconscious Zora of Eatonville before the Hegira. I feel most colored when I am thrown against a sharp white background.

For instance at Barnard. "Beside the waters of the Hudson" I feel my race. Among the thousand white

ABOVE: OLD BARN
The last rays of the day's sunshine on an ancient barn in Columbia County near Ichetucknee Springs State Park. (Photograph © Tony Arruza)

LEFT: PEACOCK ON A TIN ROOF
A peacock perches on the tin roof of an old shack near Monticello. The bone-chilling cry of the peacock was one of the songs of old Florida. (Photograph © Eric Dusenbery/ Dimensions Photography)

persons, I am a dark rock surged upon, overswept by a creamy sea. I am surged upon and overswept, but through it all, I remain myself. When covered by the waters, I am; and the ebb but reveals me again.

Sometimes it is the other way around. A white person is set down in our midst, but the contrast is just as sharp for me. For instance, when I sit in the drafty basement that is The New World Cabaret with a white person, my color comes. We enter chatting about any little nothing that we have in common and are seated by the jazz waiters. In the abrupt way that jazz orchestras have, this one plunges into a number. It loses no time in circumlocutions, but gets right down to business. It constricts the thorax and splits the heart with its tempo and narcotic harmonies. This orchestra grows rambunctious, rears on its hind legs and attacks the tonal veil with primitive fury, rending it, clawing it until it breaks through to the jungle beyond. I follow those heathen—follow them exultingly. I dance wildly inside myself; I yell within, I whoop; I shake my assegai above my head, I hurl it true to the mark *yeeeeooww!* I am in the jungle and living in the jungle way. My face is painted red and yellow, and my body is painted blue. My pulse is throbbing like a war drum. I want to slaughter something—give pain, give death to what, I do not know. But the piece ends. The men of the orchestra wipe their lips and rest their fingers. I creep back slowly to the veneer we call civilization with the last tone and find the white friend sitting motionless in his seat, smoking calmly.

"Good music they have here," he remarks, drumming the table with his fingertips.

Music! The great blobs of purple and red emotion have not touched him. He has only heard what I felt. He is far away and I see him but dimly across the ocean and the continent that have fallen between us. He is so pale with his whiteness then and I am *so* colored.

At certain times I have no race, I am *me*. When I set my hat at a certain angle and saunter down Seventh Avenue, Harlem City, feeling as snooty as the lions in front of the Forty-Second Street Library, for instance. So far as my feelings are concerned, Peggy Hopkins Joyce on the Boule Mich with her gorgeous raiment, stately carriage, knees knocking together in a most aristocratic manner, has nothing on me. The cosmic Zora emerges. I belong to no race nor time, I am the eternal feminine with its string of beads.

I have no separate feeling about being an American citizen and colored. I am merely a fragment of the Great Soul that surges within the boundaries. My country, right or wrong.

Sometimes, I feel discriminated against, but it does not make me angry. It merely astonishes me. How *can* any deny themselves the pleasure of my company! It's beyond me.

But in the main, I feel like a brown bag of miscellany propped against a wall. Against a wall in company with other bags, white, red and yellow. Pour out the contents, and there is discovered a jumble of small things priceless and worthless. A first-water diamond, an empty spool, bits of broken glass, lengths of string, a key to a door long since crumbled away, a rusty knife-blade, old shoes saved for a road that never was and never will be, a nail bent under the weight of things too heavy for any nail, a dried flower or two, still a little fragrant. In your hand is the brown bag. On the ground before you is the jumble it held—so much like the jumble in the bags, could they be emptied, that all might be dumped in a single heap and the bags refilled without altering the content of any greatly. A bit of colored glass more or less would not matter. Perhaps that is how the Great Stuffer of Bags filled them in the first place—who knows?

INDIAN PASS TRADING POST
Time passes slowly at the Indian Pass Trading Post in Gulf County. (Photograph © Eric Dusenbery/Dimensions Photography)

CHAPTER 3

The Everglades

"The general wildness, the eternal labyrinths of waters and marshes, interlocked and apparently never ending; the whole surrounded by interminable swamps. . . . Here I am then in the Floridas, thought I."
—John James Audubon,
letter to The Monthly American Journal of Geology & Natural Science, *1831*

Known as *Pay-hay-o-kee*, or "Grass-water," to the Seminole, the vast Everglades are a symbol of the uniqueness of Florida's natural wonders. The region has long been a home or refuge to Native Americans, runaway slaves, settlers, and a multitude of species of animals, reptiles, birds, and plants.

These days, the Everglades is struggling to survive. Civilization encroaches on the Grass-water and pollution destroys its life. Florida's greatest environmental challenge in the future will be the battle for the Everglades's preservation.

ABOVE: **CHOKOLOSKEE TRADING POST**
Ted Smallwood stands in the doorway of his Ole Indian Trading Post in Chokoloskee. The town was the gateway to the frontier area between the Ten Thousand Islands and the Everglades's Gulf Coast where the notorious outlaw Ed Watson once roamed. (Florida State Archives Photographic Collection)

OPPOSITE PAGE: **THE EVERGLADES**
The sun sets over Tiger Key in the Ten Thousand Islands. (Photograph © Jeff Ripple)

River of Grass

By Marjory Stoneman Douglas

When Marjory Stoneman Douglas's masterpiece, *The Everglades: River of Grass*, was first published in 1947, many people looked on the region as nothing more than an unfortunate swamp. But Douglas's writing, combined with her tireless crusade for the Everglades's conservation, brought international attention to this magnificent ecosystem.

Along with publishing her classic of nature writing, Douglas was a journalist and author of both fiction and nonfiction works, including *Road to the Sun* (1952), *Hurricane* (1958), *Alligator Crossing* (1959), *Florida: The Long Frontier* (1967), *Nine Florida Stories* (1990), and *A River in Flood and Other Florida Stories* (1998). She also fought for women's rights, racial justice, and the rights of Florida's Native Americans. When she died in 1998 at the age of 108, Florida lost one of its great citizens.

This excerpt from *The Everglades: River of Grass* is a poetic introduction to this unique wetland.

MANGROVE MAZE
Mangrove islands create a maze of trees and water in Whitewater Bay in Everglades National Park. (Photograph © Tony Arruza)

I. THE NAME

There are no other Everglades in the world.

They are, they have always been, one of the unique regions of the earth, remote, never wholly known. Nothing anywhere else is like them: their vast glittering openness, wider than the enormous visible round of the horizon, the racing free saltness and sweetness of their massive winds, under the dazzling blue heights of space. They are unique also in the simplicity, the diversity, the related harmony of the forms of life they enclose. The miracle of the light pours over the green and brown expanse of saw grass and of water, shining and slow-moving below, the grass and water that is the meaning and the central fact of the Everglades of Florida. It is a river of grass.

The great pointed paw of the state of Florida, familiar as the map of North America itself, of which it is the most noticeable appendage, thrusts south, farther south than any other part of the mainland of the United States. Between the shining aquamarine waters of the Gulf of Mexico and the roaring deep-blue waters of the north-surging Gulf Stream, the shaped land points toward Cuba and the Caribbean. It points toward and touches within one degree of the tropics.

More than halfway down that thrusting sea-bound peninsula nearly everyone knows the lake that is like a great hole in that pawing shape, Lake Okeechobee, the second largest body of fresh water, it is always said, "within the confines of the United States." Below that lie the Everglades.

They have been called "the mysterious Everglades" so long that the phrase is a meaningless platitude. For four hundred years after the discovery they seemed more like a fantasy than a simple geographic and historic fact. Even the men who in the later years saw them more clearly could hardly make up their minds what the Everglades were or how they could be described, or what use could be made of them. They were mysterious then. They are mysterious still to everyone by whom their fundamental nature is not understood.

Off and on for those four hundred years the region now called "The Everglades" was described as a series of vast, miasmic swamps, poisonous lagoons, huge dismal marshes without outlet, a rotting, shallow, inland sea, or labyrinths of dark trees bung and looped about with snakes and dripping mosses, malignant with tropical fevers and malarias, evil to the white man.

Even the name, "The Everglades," was given them and printed on a map of Florida within the past hundred years. It is variously interpreted. There were one or two other names we know, which were given them before that, but what sounds the first men had for them, seeing first, centuries and centuries before the discovering white men, those sun-blazing solitudes, we shall never know.

The shores that surround the Everglades were the first on this continent known to white men. The interior was almost the last. They have not yet been entirely mapped.

Spanish mapmakers, who never saw them, printed over the unknown blank space where they lay on those early maps the words "El Laguno del Espiritu Santo." To the early Spanish they were truly mysterious, fabulous with a wealth they were never able to prove.

The English from the Bahamas, charting the Florida coasts in the early seventeen hundreds, had no very clear idea of them. Gerard de Brahm, the surveyor, may have gone up some of the east-coast rivers and stared out on that endless, watery bright expanse, for on his map he called them "River Glades." But on the later English maps "River" becomes "Ever," so it is hard to tell what he intended.

The present name came into general use only after the acquisition of Florida from Spain in 1819 by the United States. The Turner map of 1823 was the first to use the word "Everglades." The fine Ives map of 1856 prints the words separately, "Ever Glades." In the text of the memorial that accompanied the map, they were used without capitals, as "ever glades."

The word "glade" is of the oldest English origin. It comes from the Anglo-Saxon "glaed," with the "ae" diphthong, shortened to "glad." It meant "shining" or "bright," perhaps as of water. The same word was used in the Scandinavian languages for "a clear place in the sky, a bright streak or patch of light," as Webster's International Dictionary gives it. It might even first have referred to the great openness of the sky over it, and not to the land at all.

In English for over a thousand years the word "glaed" or "glyde" or "glade" has meant an open green

SILHOUETTE AT SUNSET
The reflection of a great white heron appears like a shadow at sunset on the waters of the Everglades. (Photograph © Henry H. Holdsworth)

grassy place in the forest. And in America of the English colonies the use was continued to mean stretches of natural pasture, naturally grassy.

But most dictionaries nowadays end a definition of them with the qualifying phrase, "as of the Florida Everglades." So that they have thus become unique in being their own, and only, best definition.

Yet the Indians, who have known the Glades longer and better than any dictionary-making white men, gave them, their perfect, and poetic name, which is also true. They called them "Pa-hay-okee," which is the Indian word for "Grassy Water." Today Everglades is one word and yet plural. They are the only Everglades in the world.

Men crossed and recrossed them leaving no trace, so that no one knew men had been there. The few books or pamphlets written about them by Spaniards or surveyors or sportsmen or botanists have not been generally read. Actually, the first accurate studies of Everglades geology, soil, archaeology, even history, are only just now being completed.

The question was at once, where do you begin? Because, when you think of it, history, the recorded time of the earth and of man, is in itself something like a river. To try to present it whole is to find oneself lost in the sense of continuing change. The source can be only the beginning in time and space, and the end is the future and the unknown. What we can know lies somewhere between. The course along which for a little way one proceeds, the changing life, the varying light, must somehow be fixed in a moment clearly, from which one may look before and after and try to comprehend wholeness.

So it is with the Everglades, which have that quality of long existence in their own nature. They were changeless. They are changed.

They were complete before man came to them, and for centuries afterward, when he was only one of those forms which shared, in a finely balanced harmony, the forces and the ancient nature of the place.

Then, when the Everglades were most truly themselves, is the time to begin with them.

CYPRESS STRAND
The solitude of a cypress swamp is reflected in the marsh waters. (Photograph © Helen Longest-Saccone/Marty Saccone)

II. The Grass
The Everglades begin at Lake Okeechobee.

That is the name later Indians gave the lake, a name almost as recent as the word "Everglades." It means "Big Water." Everybody knows it.

Yet few have any idea of those pale, seemingly illimitable waters. Over the shallows, often less than a foot deep but seven hundred fifty or so square miles in actual area, the winds in one gray swift moment can shatter the reflections of sky and cloud whiteness standing still in that shining, polished, shimmering expanse. A boat can push for hours in a day of white sun through the short, crisp lake waves and there will be nothing to be seen anywhere but the brightness where the color of the water and the color of the sky become one. Men out of sight of land can stand in it up to their armpits and slowly "walk in" their long nets to the waiting boats. An everglade kite and his mate, questing in great solitary circles, rising and dipping and rising again on the wind currents, can look down all day long at the water faintly green with floating water lettuce or marked by thin standing lines of reeds, utter their sharp goat cries, and be seen and heard by no one at all.

There are great shallow islands, all brown reeds or shrubby trees thick in the water. There are masses of water weeds and hyacinths and flags rooted so long they seem solid earth, yet there is nothing but lake bottom to stand on. There the egret and the white ibis and the glossy ibis and the little blue herons in their thousands nested and circled and fed.

A long northeast wind, a "norther," can lash all that still surface to dirty vicious gray and white, over which the rain mists shut down like stained rolls of wool, so that from the eastern sand rim under dripping cypresses or the west ridge with its live oaks, no one would guess that all that waste of empty water stretched there but for the long monotonous wash of waves on unseen marshy shores.

Saw grass reaches up both sides of that lake in great enclosing arms, so that it is correct to say that the Everglades are there also. But south, southeast and southwest, where the lake water slopped and seeped and ran over and under the rock and soil, the greatest mass of the saw grass begins. It stretches as it always has stretched, in one thick enormous curving river of grass, to the very end. This is the Everglades.

It reaches one hundred miles from Lake Okeechobee to the Gulf of Mexico, fifty, sixty, even seventy miles wide. No one has ever fought his way along its full length. Few have ever crossed the northern wilderness of nothing but grass. Down that almost invisible slope the water moves. The grass stands. Where the grass and the water are there is the heart, the current, the meaning of the Everglades.

The grass and the water together make the river as simple as it is unique. There is no other river like it. Yet within that simplicity, enclosed within the river and bordering and intruding on it from each side, there is subtlety and diversity, a crowd of changing forms, of thrusting teeming life. And all that becomes the region of the Everglades.

The truth of the river is the grass. They call it saw grass. Yet in the botanical sense it is not grass at all so much as a fierce, ancient, cutting sedge. It is one of the oldest of the green growing forms in this world.

There are many places in the South where this saw grass, with its sharp central fold and edges set with fine saw teeth like points of glass, this sedge called *Cladium jamaicensis*, exists. But this is the greatest concentration of saw grass in the world. It grows fiercely in the fresh water creeping down below it. When the original saw grass thrust up its spears into the sun, the fierce sun, lord and power and first cause over the Everglades as of all the green world, then the Everglades began. They lie wherever the saw grass extends: 3,500 square miles, hundreds and thousands and millions, of acres, water and saw grass.

The first saw grass, exactly as it grows today, sprang up and lived in the sweet water and the pouring sunlight, and died in it, and from its own dried and decaying tissues and tough fibers bright with silica sprang up more fiercely again. Year after year it grew and was fed by its own brown rotting, taller and denser in the dark soil of its own death. Year after year after year, hundreds after hundreds of years, not so long as any geologic age but long in botanic time, far longer than anyone can be sure of, the saw grass grew. Four thousand years, they say, it must at least have grown like that, six feet, ten feet, twelve feet, even fifteen in places of deepest water. The edged and folded swords bristled around the delicate straight tube of pith that burst into brown flowering. The brown seed, tight enclosed after the manner of sedges, ripened in dense brownness. The seed was dropped and worked down in the water and its own ropelike mat of roots. All that decay

of leaves and seed covers and roots was packed deeper year after year by the elbowing upthrust of its own life. Year after year it laid down new layers of virgin muck under the living water.

There are places now where the depth of the muck is equal to the height of the saw grass. When it is uncovered and brought into the sunlight, its stringy and grainy dullness glitters with the myriad unrotted silica points, like glass dust.

At the edges of the Glades, and toward those southern- and southwesternmost reaches where the great estuary or delta of the Glades river takes another form entirely, the saw grass is shorter and more sparse, and the springy, porous muck deposit under it is shallower and thinner. But where the saw grass grows tallest in the deepest muck, there goes the channel of the Glades.

The water winks and flashes here and there among the sawgrass roots, as the clouds are blown across the sun. To try to make one's way among these impenetrable tufts is to be cut off from all air, to be beaten down by the sun and ripped by the grassy saw-toothed edges as one sinks in mud and water over the roots. The dried yellow stuff holds no weight. There is no earthly way to get through the mud or the standing, keen-edged blades that crowd these interminable miles.

Or in the times of high water in the old days, the flood would rise until the highest tops of that sharp grass were like a thin lawn standing out of water as blue as the sky, rippling and wrinkling, linking the pools and spreading and flowing on its true course southward.

A man standing in the center of it, if he could get there, would be as lost in saw grass, as out of sight of anything but saw grass as a man drowning in the middle of Okeechobee—or the Atlantic Ocean, for that matter—would be out of sight of land.

The water moves. The saw grass, pale green to deep-brown ripeness, stands rigid. It is moved only in sluggish rollings by the vast push of the winds across it. Over its endless acres here and there the shadows of the dazzling clouds quicken and slide, purple-brown, plum-brown, mauve-brown, rust-brown, bronze. The bristling, blossoming tops do not bend easily like

SUNSET

The sun drops behind the clouds above Paurotis Pond in the Everglades. (Photograph © Helen Longest-Saccone/Marty Saccone)

standing grain. They do not even in their own growth curve all one way but stand in edged clumps, curving against each other, all the massed curving blades making millions of fine arching lines that at a little distance merge to a huge expanse of brown wires or bristles or, farther beyond, to deep-piled plush. At the horizon they become velvet. The line they make is an edge of velvet against the infinite blue, the blue-and-white, the clear fine primrose yellow, the burning brass and crimson, the molten silver, the deepening hyacinth sky.

The clear burning light of the sun pours daylong into the saw grass and is lost there, soaked up, never given back. Only the water flashes and glints. The grass yields nothing.

Nothing less than the smashing power of some hurricane can beat it down. Then one can see, from high up in a plane, where the towering weight and velocity of the hurricane was the strongest and where along the edges of its whorl it turned less and less savagely and left the saw grass standing. Even so, the grass is not flattened in a continuous swath but only here and here and over there, as if the storm bounced or lifted and smashed down again in great hammering strokes or enormous cat-licks.

Only one force can conquer it completely and that is fire. Deep in the layers of muck there are layers of ashes, marks of old fires set by lightning or the early Indians. But in the early days the water always came back and there were long slow years in which the saw grass grew and died, laying down again its tough resilient decay.

This is the saw grass, then, which seems to move as the water moved, in a great thick arc south and southwestward from Okeechobee to the Gulf. There at the last imperceptible incline of the land the saw grass goes along the headwaters of many of those wide, slow, mangrove-bordered fresh-water rivers, like a delta or an estuary into which the salt tides flow and draw back and flow again.

The mangrove becomes a solid barrier there, which by its strong, arched and labyrinthine roots collects the sweepage of the fresh water and the salt and holds back the parent sea. The supple branches, the oily green leaves, set up a barrier against the winds, although the hurricanes prevail easily against them. There the fresh water meets the incoming salt, and is lost.

It may be that the mystery of the Everglades is the saw grass, so simple, so enduring, so hostile. It was the saw grass and the water which divided east coast from west coast and made the central solitudes that held in them the secrets of time, which has moved here so long unmarked.

III. The Water
In the Everglades one is most aware of the superb monotony of saw grass under the world of air. But below that and before it, enclosing and causing it, is the water.

It is poured into Lake Okeechobee from the north and west, from that fine chain of lakes which scatter up and down the center of Florida, like bright beads from a string. They overflow southward. The water is gathered from the northwest through a wide area of open savannas and prairies. It swells the greatest contributing streams, the Kissimmee River, and the Taylor River and Fisheating Creek, and dozens of other smaller named and unnamed creeks or rivulets, and through them moves down into the great lake's tideless blue-misted expanse.

The water comes from the rains. The northern lakes and streams, Okeechobee itself, are only channels and reservoirs and conduits for a surface flow of rain water, fresh from the clouds. A few springs may feed them, but no melting snow water, no mountain freshets, no upgushing from caverns in ancient rock. Here the rain is everything.

Here the rain falls more powerfully and logically than anywhere else upon the temperate mainland of the United States. There are not four sharply marked seasons, as in the North. Here winter and spring and summer and fall blend into each other subtly, with nothing like such extremes of heat and cold. Here, actually, there are only two seasons, the wet and the dry, as there are in the tropics. The rains thunder over all this long land in their appointed season from the low clouds blowing in from the sea, or pour from clouds gathered all morning from the condensation of the wet below. Then for months it will not rain at all, or very little, and the high sun glares over the drying saw grass and the river seems to stand still.

This land, by the maps, is in the temperate zone. But the laws of the rain and of the seasons here are tropic laws.

The men who make maps draw lines across seas

and deserts and mountains and equatorial rain forests to show where the Temperate Zone is cut off sharply from the middle equatorial belt. But the sea and the land and the winds do not always recognize that rigidity. Nor do southern Florida and the Everglades.

To the west the map shows the Gulf of Mexico, that warm land-sheltered, almost inland ocean; and from it, moved by the power of the turning world itself, the Gulf Stream pours its warm deep indigo and white-flecked waters north of Cuba and ever northeastward. "The Stream" is a huge swift-running river of warm salt water forced between the Florida coast, which it has shaped, and the Bahama banks, until high up on the blue globe of ocean it swings far across into the gray latitudes, toward frozen seas.

With all that surrounding warm sea water and not forgetting Okeechobee's over seven hundred shallow watery square miles, east forty miles from the sea, and from the Gulf eighty, the whole southern part of Florida might as well be an island.

ABOVE: **RIVER OF GRASS**
Stalks of saw grass stretch to the horizon. The Everglades were known as Pay-hay-o-kee, *or "Grass-water," to the Seminole. (Photograph © Maresa Pryor)*

OVERLEAF: **MANGROVE AND OYSTERS**
At low tide, a red mangrove and a multitude of oysters appear to be marooned by the waters of the Everglades in the Ten Thousand Islands. (Photograph © Jeff Ripple)

A Life in the Everglades

By Loren G. "Totch" Brown

Loren G. "Totch" Brown made his life in the wilds of the Everglades, particularly among the Ten Thousand Islands along the Gulf Coast. He worked as an alligator hunter, crabber, poacher, guide, commercial fisherman, marijuana runner, and whatever else he needed to do to survive.

Brown wrote an autobiography of a forgotten way of life in *Totch: A Life in the Everglades* (1993). As Peter Matthiessen explained in his foreword, "Totch Brown's lively memoirs of vanished days in the Ten Thousand Islands—the last real frontier in Florida—are invaluable as well as entertaining." Brown was a link back to old Florida and the infamous renegade outlaw Ed Watson, whom Matthiessen wrote of in his own trilogy of novels *Killing Mister Watson* (1990), *Lost Man's River* (1997), and *Bone By Bone* (1999).

This excerpt from Brown's memoirs introduces his haunts and bygone days.

❧

GATOR
An American alligator casts a wary eye in the Everglades. (Photograph © Tony Arruza)

FROM SCRATCHING OUT a living as an alligator-hunter and commercial fisherman to smuggling marijuana from Colombia to the hidden waters of Florida's Ten Thousand Islands: that's just the beginning and end of this story. The most interesting part, to my opinion, comes in between: the frontier style of life I lived in the untamed Everglades. The islands, a part of the Glades, are located along Florida's southwest Gulf coast, a "country" like no other place in the United States.

That way of living—free but hard—started for my family in 1880, when my paternal great-grandfather, John J. Brown, settled here on Florida's last frontier. Soon after, my maternal grandfather, Charles G. McKinney, came to the frontier and started a forty-year career as midwife, dentist, storekeeper, and sage.

Along with the pioneers came a desperado named Ed J. Watson in the 1890s, who claimed he'd killed the woman outlaw Belle Starr in Oklahoma, and was on the run from her lover, Jesse James. Whether he did or he didn't, he bloodied the water around the Islands, making believers out of many who didn't live to tell it. Outlaws like Watson were followed by lesser lawbreakers—plume-hunters, bank robbers, and when Prohibition came along in the 1920s, moonshiners and rumrunners.

For nearly a century it was a challenging and rewarding way of life. But as time rocked on, changes in the Everglades made it hard to earn a living fishing or hunting—so hard that by the 1970s many good family men got around to feeling that to survive, they'd just have to break the law themselves, or leave the country.

That's when the Glades and the Islands became a marijuana smuggler's paradise, and when my own way of life changed completely. Instead of stone crab or mackerel, I loaded my seventy-two-foot shrimp boat in Colombia with all the pot she'd float with, and drove 'er home across the Caribbean. Until then I'd thought hunting alligators up to fourteen foot, with some of 'em coming at me head-on, was scary enough, but the fright that came with pot-hauling would scare a full-grown tomcat out of all nine of his lives. Along with the frights, though, came experiences so exciting they'd make a sick man well.

All the same, hauling marijuana wasn't really my way of life. It was a means of survival when the chips were down. But the life I lived in the Everglades as a gator-hunter and commercial fisherman is an altogether different story. It was a way of surviving against odds as heavy as they come, in a country my forefathers made their own—a way of life that is probably gone forever.

While life in the Everglades was no picnic, the privilege of living a free life that close to nature was worth all the hardships that came with it: coping with alligators, panthers, and rattlesnakes on muddy lands filled with poison ivy, spiders, and mosquitoes so thick you could rake 'em off your brow by the handful. In 1934, when I was fourteen, times got so hard I quit school and started working full-time. By the time I was thirteen I had my own small motorboat for hunting (one of the few around). As a teenager I fought my way through the Great Depression hunting raccoons and alligators. By age seventeen I owned a commercial fishing boat and was captain of my own crew. Commercial fishing was both exciting and hard, sweating out eighteen-hour workdays and storms at sea.

Then came World War II, and I became a combat infantryman, fighting my way through the Battle of the Bulge. Only this time, instead of fighting the elements for survival, it was man-to-man combat fighting for my life. When I came back from overseas, my homeland soon became the Everglades National Park and my way of life became a fight all over again, having to outrun the park rangers and the Coast Guard on the high seas.

With a life like that, I felt the only way to do it right was for me to tell it in my own style, slang and grammar included. So as my memory goes back and

While my writing is on the flow,
I'm going to write as though
I'm still in the Everglades
    as hard as I can go—
Not only writing history
But reliving it for you.

"The country" is made up of a group of mangrove keys known as the Ten Thousand Islands, laying along Florida's southwest coast. A narrow strip maybe five miles wide of low mangrove mainland separates the Islands from the western Everglades. Both the Islands and the Glades are too low to live on except for about forty small oyster-shell island mounds probably built by the Calusa Indians or some other early settlers, the

GATOR HUNTER
An old-time gator hunter poses with his prey. On this 1920 hunt, thirty alligators were taken, ranging in size from twelve inches to twelve feet in length. (Florida State Archives Photographic Collection)

CYPRESS SCULPTURES
Bald cypress trees in the Everglades catch the last light of the day in their branches. (Photograph © Maresa Pryor)

books say before Christ. The mounds are two to twenty feet above sea level, ranging in size from fifty feet across to 150 acres, with Chokoloskee (pronounced Chuck-a-luskee) being the largest.

Chokoloskee Island and Everglades City are located eighty miles west of Miami just off the Tamiami Trail (U.S. 41) on State Road 29, the western gateway to the Everglades National Park. Until 1956, when a four-mile causeway was built out from Everglades City, the only way to reach the island was by boat.

In Chokoloskee's early years the only way to trade or communicate with the outside world was by sailboat to Key West. The first settlers had but few choices on how to go about making a living. In the winter months they hunted for raccoons and pretty much the year around for alligators.

There were plenty of fish, especially mullet, and for shipping out they were salted, no ice. Loggerhead turtles were kept alive on the deck of the boat. Large clams were more than plentiful and so were oysters (a little salt water kept them alive). Grandfather McKinney wrote that the Key West pet market paid up to $1.25 each for redbirds, and a good price for swallow-tailed kite eggs (used for what, I can't imagine).

Vegetables played a big part in survival in those

pioneer days. The shell islands in this country are not exactly mounds, as they're often called, but more like a hilly field or a ridge, with enough soil on top of the shell in places to grow most anything. Sugarcane grew like wild, and after being made into syrup, it was shipped out by the barrel—also the cane itself, for chewing. The stores weren't full of candy bars and the kids' pockets weren't full of quarters; a piece of sweet cane to chew on went pretty good.

The Islands were rich in fruit—guavas, sugar apples, sweet and sour oranges, limes, grapefruit, papaya, plenty of avocado pears—and there was always a good market for them. After reaching Key West much of the produce was shipped to New York by way of steam ships.

In trading, firewood probably played one of the biggest roles (remember, back then heating wasn't push-button like it is today). There's a good firewood in this country called buttonwood, similar to oak or hickory; it sold at three dollars a cord (128 cubic feet). The old-timers cut several cords a day with an ax and handsaw. Today it might be hard to find a man physically able to cut enough buttonwood for a good campfire.

Getting food from the land was no problem, especially for the hunters. The waters were running over with fish, and the Glades and Islands were filled with wildlife, from deer to saltwater birds, that made great eating. There were usually a few cows around, but really more for milk than for meat.

Living in those pioneer days took strong men and women—many people would never have made it, not even in my time. Most of the houses were more like shacks, built out of anything from tin to palmetto fans and set up on buttonwood posts cut from the swamp, with wooden shutters or a sheet of tin or canvas for windows. The only lights were kerosene and carbide miner's lamps, for the home as well as for hunting and fishing at night. All cooking was done on a wood or kerosene stove or over an open fire.

There was no such thing as a bathroom or bathtub back then or for a long time after. For bathing, most of us used a galvanized tin washtub and a couple of buckets of rainwater caught from the roof; the women and children bathed first. The toilet was an outhouse in the back if you were lucky; otherwise, a log in the bushes to hunker down on. (I knew some people who once used a log from a poisonous tree

SEMINOLE MAN WITH UMBRELLA
Seminole Jimmie Tiger stands proudly with his umbrella in this studio portrait from the 1930s. (Florida State Archives Photographic Collection)

called the manchineel—worse than poison ivy. You can guess what happened when they hunkered down on that.) Toilet paper was a rare thing, hardly ever for sale on the island. The story goes that sometime in the 1930s, a tourist stopped by Ted Smallwood's store to buy some toilet paper (my Uncle Harry Brown called it "bathroom stationery"). "No stock," Ted told the tourist. "Get yourself a mangrove root with barnacles on it. That's what we use around here."

Homage to a Magical Place

By Carl Hiaasen

These days, Carl Hiaasen is a household name among mystery buffs. The fans of his many books—from *Tourist Season* (1986), *Strip Tease* (1993), and *Stormy Weather* (1995) to his latest, *Sick Puppy* (2000)—have made Hiaasen a best-selling author.

Hiaasen first made a name for himself, however, as a newspaper reporter and columnist, and since 1985 he has penned some 1,300 columns for the *Miami Herald*. As he says of his brand of old-school journalism, "You just cover a lot of territory and you do it aggressively and you do it fairly and you don't play favorites and you don't take any prisoners. It's the old school of slash-and-burn metropolitan column writing. You just kick ass. That's what you do. And that's what they pay you to do."

The thread running throughout all of Hiaasen's writing—whether it's his mysteries or his newspaper work—is a scrappy spirit willing to fight to preserve Florida's natural world. This column, a prime example of that theme, was first published in the *Herald* on October 19, 1997, to celebrate the fiftieth anniversary of the Everglades National Park.

EGRETS
A trio of juvenile great egrets. (Photograph © Helen Longest-Saccone/Marty Saccone)

THE CABIN HUNG on wooden stilts in a marsh pond, the stilts rising up through lily pads as big as hubcaps.

Getting there was tricky but my friends Andy and Matt knew the way—gunning a johnboat down subtle and sinuous trails, the sawgrass whisking against the hull. If you were foolish enough to stick out your hand, it came back bleeding.

The stalks were so high and thick that they parted like a curtain when we plowed through. The boat's bow acted as a scoop, picking up gem-green chameleons and ribbon snakes and leopard frogs. By the time we reached the cabin, we'd usually have spider webs on our heads, and sometimes the spiders themselves.

We were kids, and it was fantastic. It was the Everglades.

One night we stood on the canted porch and watched tiny starbursts of color in the distant sky. At first we couldn't figure out what they were, and then we remembered: it was the Fourth of July. Those were fireworks over the city of Fort Lauderdale.

But we were so far away that all we could hear was the peeping of frogs and the hum of mosquitoes and the occasional trill of an owl. We didn't need to be told it was a magical place. We didn't need to be reminded how lucky we were.

I don't know if the old shack is still standing in Conservation Area 2B, but the eastward view certainly isn't the same. Instead of starlight you now get the glow from the Sawgrass Mills mall, a humongous Ford dealership and, absurdly, the crown of a new pro hockey arena.

We wouldn't have thought it possible, three teenagers gazing across wild country that swept to all horizons. Ice hockey on the doorstep of the Everglades! We couldn't have imagined such soulless incongruity and blithering greed.

Fortunately, somebody was smarter than we were. Somebody 30 years earlier had realized that the most imposing of natural wonders, even a river of grass, could be destroyed if enough well-financed intruders set their minds to it.

And somebody also understood that Dade, Broward and Palm Beach counties would inevitably grow westward as haphazardly as fungus, and with even less regard for their mother host.

So that, politically, the only part of the Everglades that could be set aside for true preservation was its remote southernmost spur, and not without a battle. As impenetrable as the area appeared, speculators nonetheless mulled ways to log it, plow it, mine it or subdivide it.

That the U.S. Congress and state Legislature ever went along with the idea of an Everglades National Park remains astounding, 50 years after its dedication.

Nature helped its own cause. Hurricanes hammered South Florida in the 1930s and 1940s, so most land grabbers weren't in the market for more submerged acreage. It was hard enough hawking the soggy, stamp-sized lots they already had.

Seasonal flooding and fires had become such a threat to coastal development that extravagant technology was being directed toward a radical solution: containing and controlling all water near the farms and newly sprouted towns.

EVERGLADES STAMP
To pay homage to the creation of the Everglades National Park, the U.S. Post Office Department (later the U.S. Postal Service) issued this stamp, postmarked here in Florida City on the first day of issue, December 5, 1947.

MORNING MIST
The sun rises through the morning mist at Anhinga Trail in the Everglades. (Photograph © Maresa Pryor)

SUNRISE
The sun rises over the waters of Florida Bay. (Photograph © Helen Longest-Saccone/Marty Saccone)

Thus preoccupied, most entrepreneurs remained wary of the buggy, moccasin-infested wetlands below the Tamiami Trail. That particular wilderness was, if not unconquerable, presumed not worth the high cost of conquering.

So in 1947 there came to be a spectacular national park, 1.3 million acres and destined to grow.

Ironically, it wasn't long afterwards that the rest of the Everglades, an area five times the size of the park, came under attack from the dredge and the bull-dozer—a methodical and arrogant replumbing. Hundreds of miles of canals and dikes were gouged through the sawgrass meadows, pond apple sloughs and cypress heads.

Once the big "water management" project got under way, not enough people considered what might happen to the park itself, to the south. Too few understood its vascular, life-or-death connection to the sugarcane fields of Clewiston, the limerock mines of Medley or the tomato farms of Homestead.

As a consequence, hundreds of millions of dollars are today being requisitioned to undo the damage and "restore" both the flow and purity of the Everglades. Nowhere in the world has such a massive, complex hydrological repair been attempted. If by some miracle it succeeds, your children and their children probably will never run out of clean water.

And, as a fine bonus, they might get to see a healthier Everglades National Park.

As vulnerable and anemic as it is, the park remains impressive and occasionally awesome; still rightfully mentioned in the same breath with Yellowstone and Grand Canyon.

Visually, its beauty is of an inverse dimension, for the Glades are as flat as a skillet, the trees mostly tangled and scrubby, the waters slow and dark. The monotony of its landscape can be a deception, as endless and uninviting as arctic tundra.

But for anyone finding themselves on that long two-lane road to Flamingo when the sun comes up, there's no place comparable in the universe.

True, the Everglades have no regal herds of elk or buffalo to halt tourist traffic—you might briefly be delayed by a box turtle plodding across the blacktop, or by a homely opossum. Yet for the matchless diversity of its inhabitants, the park is truly unique.

That's because it is essentially the tailing-out of a great temperate river, transformed on its southerly glide from freshwater prairies to an immense salty estuary, Florida Bay.

Entering by canoe at Shark River, you would be among woodpeckers and mockingbirds, alligators and bullfrogs, garfish and bass, whitetailed deer and possibly otters. Most of them you wouldn't see, but they'd be there.

And by the time you finished paddling—at Cape Sable or Snake Bight or the Ten Thousand Islands—you would have also been among roseate spoonbills and white pelicans, eels and mangrove snakes, sawfish and redfish and crusty loggerhead turtles.

Buffaloes are grand, but name another park that harbors panthers at one end and hammerhead sharks at the other. Name another park where, on a spring morning, it's possible to encounter bald eagles, manatees, a jewfish the size of a wine cask, an indigo snake as rare as sapphire, and even a wild pink flamingo.

I feel blessed because the park's southern boundary reaches practically to my back door. One June evening, I walked the shore of a mangrove bay and counted four crocodile nests; in a whole lifetime most Floridians will never lay eyes on one. Another afternoon, in July, I helped tag and release a young green turtle, a seldom-seen species that once teetered toward extinction.

And only weeks ago, near Sandy Key, I saw a pod of bottle-nosed dolphins doing spectacular back-flips for no other reason but the joy of it. Nobody was there to applaud or snap pictures; the dolphins were their own best audience, exactly as it ought to have been.

Such moments are remarkable if you consider what has happened to the rest of South Florida in the past half a century. It seems miraculous that the Everglades haven't been completely parched, poached or poisoned to stagnation by the six million people who've moved in around them.

The more who come, the more important the national park becomes—not only as a refuge for imperiled wildlife but as a symbolic monument for future human generations; one consecrated place that shows somebody down here cared, somebody understood, somebody appreciated.

A fantastic place from which your children and their children will, if they're lucky, never see the lights of an outlet mall or a car lot or a ridiculous hockey stadium. Just starburst glimpses of birds and baby gators and high-flying dolphins.

An old-time fishing shack stands high above the Gulf Coast's tranquil waters off North Captiva Island at sunrise. (Photograph © Helen Longest-Saccone/Marty Saccone)

CHAPTER 4

Vacationland, U.S.A.

"And though the days of faith be dead, men look for that Phantom-Fountain still. Yearly, from the cities of wintry lands thousands hasten to the eternal summer of this perfumed place, to find new life, new strength—to seek rejuvenescence in the balm of the undying groves, in the purity of rock-born springs, in the elixir-breath of this tropical Nature, herself eternally young with the luminous youth of the gods. And multitudes pass away again to duller lands, to darker skies, rejuvenated indeed,—the beauty with rose-bloom brightened, the toiler with force renewed,—feeling they have left behind them here something of their hearts, something of their souls, caught like Spanish moss on the spiked leaves of the palms, on the outstretched arms of the cedars."
—*Lafcadio Hearn,* Floridian Reveries, *1911*

People have long journeyed from northern climes to Florida in search of sun and fun to refresh their spirits. Whether they are seeking a Fountain of Youth, a Garden of Eden, a land of enchantment, or a snowbird's retreat from winter, Florida has become Vacationland, U.S.A.

Above: **"Vivacious Florida"**
Greetings from the "Year-'round Vacation-land" in this 1940s postcard pack.

Opposite Page: **Starfish**
Waves sweep Pensacola Beach, washing over a lone starfish at the water's edge. (Photograph © Maresa Pryor)

On the Florida Beach

In Camp at Sarasota Florida.
May - 9th 1929.

TYPICAL DOUBLE BED ROOM

TYPICAL TWIN-BED ROOM

SHAW'S MOTOR COURT

OFFICE

A VIEW OF SHAW'S MOTOR COURT - ON U. S. 41

The Tin Canners

By David A. Thornburg

Palm Beach, St. Petersburg, and other hot spots attracted the rich and famous, or at least the well-to-do. But regular folk also made the pilgrimage to Florida, starting as part of a craze in the 1920s, when a mass of humanity, known somewhat derisively as the "Tin Canners," drove south for a little R & R. The newfangled automobile gave people a means to travel, and the strange invention then known as the "house trailer" provided a home away from home.

David A. Thornburg was born in a house trailer during this craze. He later researched and wrote *Galloping Bungalows: The Rise and Demise of the American House Trailer* (1991), a thoroughly entertaining and enlightening blend of cultural and technical history highlighted by a great sense for storytelling and witty prose.

This excerpt from *Galloping Bungalows* describes the rise of the Tin Canners that laid the groundwork for many Florida vacationers since.

TIN CANNERS
Florida's sunshine and beaches attracted tourists like moths to a candle. Whether rich or poor, all wanted a taste of the sea air and the warm clime.

LONG BEFORE WORLD War I, and long before the advent of national weather reports, rumors of Florida's winter climate crept northward to haunt the snowbound Yankee:

"Heard it was eighty-two degrees one day last week down in Miami."

"Hell you say! What is it out there now?"

"Can't see for the frost on the window . . . looks like eight below."

"Huh! If we was Rocky-fellers, I reckon we'd be in Miami."

And of course they were in Miami—the Rocky-fellers, that is. They slipped away just after Christmas, by steam yacht, by ocean liner, by "private varnish," those exotic and hand-crafted Pullman cars of the very rich, long and sleek and servant-encrusted, with discreetly drawn shades and names like "Pilgrim" and "Idlehour" printed in gilt letters on their forest-green sides. Cars that were coupled quietly and unobtrusively to the rear of southbound express trains just as they were leaving the station.

They arrived with little fanfare, these Rocky-fellers. They stayed at Florida's best hotels, they ate shrimp bernaise and oysters Rockefeller in her most elegant restaurants. They played golf and tennis at her swankiest spas. And then, tanned and rejuvenated, they melted away again in April or May, to return to their money factories in the North. The state of Florida had been invented by the rich for the rich, and in the three decades prior to World War I, the rich had their new invention pretty much to themselves.

Then came the motorcar—in vast numbers. In 1910, America had fewer than half a million automobiles; ten years later the figure had risen to something over eight million—one vehicle for every dozen citizens: man, woman, and child. Tall and gawky and fragile and cantankerous they were, but what a piece of unthinkable magic! What a machine for annihilating distance! To own one was to own seven-league boots . . . to have wings on your heels . . . to hold the reins of Pegasus. Who could hold the reins of Pegasus without craving to go for a ride?

And ride they did. On weekends, on holidays, on vacations, this daring and dust-covered generation of postwar Americans ventured out further and further in their rickety machines, bouncing along two-hundred-year-old wagon ruts, popping and wheezing down hopelessly muddy lanes, fording creeks in creaking Fords, and getting further from home on a casual Sunday afternoon drive than their parents had gone for their honeymoon.

"Heard it was eighty-two degrees one day last week down in Miami."

"Hell you say—let's go give her a look-see. . . ."

Suddenly the states below the snowline found themselves host to a whole new class of winter tourist, more numerous and less quiet than the folk who had come by yacht and private pullman. More numerous and less quiet—and nowhere near as rich.

These new tourists didn't come south to stay at

Winter Bathing at Miami Beach, Miami, Fla.

the fancy hotels and resorts, and they didn't come to eat shrimp bernaise and oysters Rockefeller in the elegant restaurants. They came popping and wheezing down U.S. Highway One with tents tied to their muddy running boards, with pots and pans and gasoline campstoves piled in the back seat; pots and pans and gasoline campstoves, and folding chairs and collapsible cots and inflatable mattresses and forty-pound boxes of dirt containing live fishing worms. Never having been so far from their own kitchens, and unsure of what to expect in the way of provisions on the road, they loaded their Fords and Moons and Dodges and battered old Franklin touring cars with canned meat and canned vegetables and even canned fruit— *they brought their own fruit to Florida.* The great American motor-camping craze had begun.

It didn't take long for the locals to size up these new visitors, to get them stereotyped to satisfaction:

"I s'pose you heard about th' Yankee that come south fer th' winter with one clean shirt an' a ten-dollar bill, an' never changed neither one. . . ."

"They drive tin cans and they eat outa tin cans and they leave a trail of tin cans behind 'em. They're tin-can tourists, that's what they are."

Tin can tourists. The label wasn't particularly fair, for the cars and the eating habits of these nouveau gypsies were, on the whole, no tinnier than anyone else's. But the phrase had a nasty ring to it, and it stuck. It appealed especially to real estate salesmen and hotel keepers and restaurant owners, all of whom were heartily sick of seeing carloads of these strangers go gawking and pointing past their door, in search of a stretch of open beach, a vacant lot, an unfenced schoolyard to pound their tent stakes into for the night.

"Just lookit them fools! Don't they know that all that land out there belongs to somebody? They're just freeloaders, ever one of 'em—nothin' but a buncha damn tin canners!"

Now condescension of this sort is cheap and easy, and it can be a great comfort to the condescender. But it takes two to play the game. What happens if the object of your scorn doesn't care a whit for your opinion? Suppose he refuses to see himself as your inferior—just laughs at your sneers, makes a joke of the names you call him?

And that's exactly what those damned infuriating Yankees did. Those *tin can tourists* in their stinking, noisy, overloaded, mud-covered flivvers simply refused to be intimidated. In their hearts and in their tents they knew they were the social equals of the realtors and hotel keepers and restaurant owners who derided them—if for no other reason, because so many of them were themselves realtors and hotel and restaurant owners back home. They weren't gypsies and they weren't freeloaders, and they knew it. They were sub-

January Swim
Drawing droves of tourists to Florida were images such as this, showing the sun, sand, and surf on a fine January day in 1921 when the swimming was good. (Library of Congress)

stantial middle-class Americans (maybe even a cut above average—hell's bells, they owned motorcars, didn't they?) who were out looking for a change of scenery and a breath of fresh air and a little adventure and good fellowship under the stars. Why, dammit, they were motor campers! Didn't those crazy crackers read *Popular Science* and *The Saturday Evening Post*? Didn't they know there was a fad going on?

And so, when it came time to organize all this adventure and good fellowship, to create for themselves a kind of Elks lodge of the open road, the motor campers had no trouble choosing a name for their club. They would be the Tin Can Tourists of America—the TCT.

Their founder was a genial chap from Chicago named James M. Morrison. A veteran motor camper himself, Morrison planted the idea for the club among some twenty-two families camped in Tampa's De Soto Park in December of 1919. Within two months they were chartered; an organization with "no fees, no dues, no graft," whose motto was the Golden Rule. If Morrison and his fellow-founders had any social or political aims—to fight for better highways, say, or more government campgrounds, or fewer signs in schoolyards that said "no tourists allowed"—these aims were conspicuously absent from the club charter, which merely hoped "to unite fraternally all auto campers; to establish a feeling of friendship among them and a friendly basis with local residents; to provide clean and wholesome entertainment in camps and at meetings; to spread the gospel of cleanliness in all camps, as well as enforce rules governing all camp grounds; to put out all campfires, destroy no property, and purloin nothing; to help a fellow member in distress on the road without injury to one's self or car."

And how was one to recognize fellow members in distress on the road? Simple; their cars would be displaying the proud badge of the TCT, an empty soup can dangling from the radiator cap. Total strangers, sailing past one another with cans at full mast, would hail each other like brothers. Often they'd heave to and trade road information, using license plates in lieu of names: "Say there, New York—how much farther to Steubenville?" When they parted, still without exchanging names, it was with a hearty "seeya at convention!" The Tin Can Tourists.

Their winter convention was in Tampa, usually in late January or early February. Summer Convention,

in August, would be in some cool, shady spot "up north." The main business of Winter Convention was to decide when and where Summer Convention was to be held, and vice versa. And to vote in a new "Royal Can Opener"—their chief executive officer—for the coming year, and announce the winner of the day's horseshoe tournament, while speculating on how the shoes might fall for the various players the next day. Then might come a few rousing group songs, including three or four repetitions of the official theme song of the TCT:

> The more we get together,
>> Together, together,
> The more we get together,
> The happier we'll be.
>> For your friends are my friends
>> And my friends are your friends,
> The more we get together,
>> The happier we'll be.

The tin canners. They went popping and wheezing and tenting and singing their merry way right through the Roaring Twenties, making converts left and right, for every member was empowered to swear in new Canners on the spot, wherever their trails might cross—no fees, no dues, no graft—and invite them to the next convention. Within a decade TCT membership had grown to almost 100 thousand—estimated, of course, because no one kept written records.

The tin canners. Hadn't they read Sinclair Lewis, Hemingway, Scott Fitzgerald? Weren't they aware that they were glad handing their way right through the Jazz Age, the Age of Cynicism? Did they have any idea what scorn H. L. Mencken would have heaped on their innocent and homely little boy scout charter, their secret handshake (a sawing motion), secret sign (a "C" made with the thumb and forefinger), or secret password ("nit nac")? Did they stop to think of what the sharp-tongued Dorothy Parker might have made of a group of adults—total strangers for the most part—crouched about a campfire in shirt-sleeves, popping their old-fashioned galluses and singing

> The more we get together,
> Together, together. . . .

Did they care? For every Sinclair Lewis there are probably a thousand Babbits—a ratio that seems to work out about right for everybody involved.

The tin canners. Like most Americans, like most people, they disliked the continual change they saw going on all around them. They were suspicious of all this progress, progress, progress. They idealized the past and looked with suspicion upon the future. The past, in their minds, was simple and easygoing and folksy— Arcadian. The past was the golden age of friendliness and camaraderie among strong, free, independent, self-sufficient people. The past was classless and democratic. And most of all, the past was rural.

This was their myth, their dream, their Holy Grail.

Every summer they went out on the highway in search of it. They packed their bedrolls and cranked up their Tin Lizzies and puttered off looking for the past. And— as so often happens—what they found instead was the future. For the Tin Can Tourists of the twenties, with their auto camps and their sweet dream of Arcady, quite literally paved the way for the house trailer revolution of the following decade.

How to Retire to Florida

By George and Jane Dusenbury

At the beginning of the 1500s, Caribbean natives are said to have guided Spaniard Ponce de Léon to the peninsula that would become Florida with word of a spring whose waters restored youth. Since then, explorers and vacationers alike have ventured to Florida in search of the Fountain of Youth—or at least relaxation and restoration on the beaches of the Sunshine State.

George and Jane Dusenbury published their popular guidebook *How to Retire to Florida* in 1947. Catching the crest of a wave, the duo offered advice to potential snowbirds on making "a fresh start in Florida." The book aided newcomers in everything from choosing a "section" of Florida, recommendations on real estate, an overview of trailer-camp life, and advice on budgeting for retirement. The final part of the book offered sunny case studies of people who were happy with their new Florida home.

This introduction to Florida retirement made seeking out a new life in Florida hard to resist for many retirees.

GOLDEN SUNSHINE
An advertising poster for Miami from the 1920s promises "golden sunshine adds golden years."

THE DAY YOU retire you either enter your decline, or make a fresh start in life. There is no in-between. The unalterable law of life is "grow or go."

Where you now live, the chief concern of life is the pursuit of money; a "living" means "an income."

Thus the day you stop going to work you start drifting away from the main stream of your community's life—away from friends, interests, activities. Of course, lying abed mornings is a wonderful novelty at first. So are all-day radio sessions when the weather is bad—and golf and gardening when it isn't. But it will hurt when you discover that you have less and less in common with people in your business community.

Staying where you are after you retire means a *decline*—lower income in relationship to the community, less activity, fewer friends, diminished interest—a drying up and dying of your life force. You've seen it happen many times—and, of course, you've seen exceptions. But in the vast majority of cases, the man who retires where he has worked becomes a "has been." Almost everything is stacked against him.

While there is a great temptation to let things drift when you retire—to sit back and relax where you are—there also is a temptation to make a clean break with the past and get off to a fresh start. One of the deepest longings of a human being is to start all over again in new circumstances, out of his old ruts, away from the pigeon-holes people have put him in, out from under the shadow of past failures associated with people and places.

The best place to make a fresh start after retirement, in our opinion, is Florida. One reason for this is its "differentness." But it is that very factor of differentness—in the form of fear of the unknown—that keeps so many people from climaxing their lives in Florida. To change that unknown to a known is the central purpose of this book.

If you have never given Florida particular thought, perhaps it's in the back of your mind as a sunny peninsula covered stem to stern with waving coconut palms, and populated with bathing girls, rich tourists and race horses.

Well, it *is* sunny.

And the coconut palms are lovely in the fraction of the state where they do wave.

But there are thousands of people there like you populating the state in good measure. The only bathing girls they are interested in are their visiting granddaughters. The rich tourists they may not even note in passing, and the race horses they see in the newsreel.

ANGLING DUO
A great white heron waits patiently to see what the day's catch might bring on Sanibel Island. (Photograph © Lynn M. Stone)

St.Petersburg
FLORIDA

The Sunshine City

"The Sunshine City"
As in many other Florida cities, the St. Petersburg chamber of commerce issued detailed brochures such as this one from the 1920s inviting all and sundry to their corner of paradise. As this flyer read, "With the flush of dawn in Florida comes the cheerful serenade of the mocking bird, bidding you to arise and live . . . for the beginning of a new day in the Sunshine City is like a journey to a new world."

The Tourist Invasion Described

By Authors of the Federal Writers' Project

The Federal Writers' Project's 1939 guide to Florida offered an amusing—albeit largely true—portrait of the average tourist.

Across the wide strip of its upper area, from the Atlantic to within a short distance of the Mississippi border, Florida is at once a continuation of the Deep South and the beginning of a new realm in which the system of two-party politics reasserts itself. Narrowing abruptly to a peninsula, it drops through five degrees of latitude and a constantly accentuated tropical setting, until the tip of its long Roman nose pokes very nearly into the confines and atmosphere of Latin America. Equatorial waters move up from the south along its coasts, to temper its climate and confuse its seasons; every winter a tidal wave of tourists moves down from the north, to affect its culture, its economy, its physical appearance. Throughout more than four centuries, from Ponce de Leon in his caravels to the latest Pennsylvanian in his Buick, Florida has been invaded by seekers of gold or of sunshine; yet it has retained an identity and a character distinctive to itself. The result of all this is a material and immaterial pattern of infinite variety, replete with contrasts, paradoxes, confusions, and inconsistencies.

Politically and socially, Florida has its own North and South, but its northern area is strictly southern and its southern area definitely northern. In summer the State is predominantly southern by birth and adoptions, and in winter it is northern by invasion. . . .

The signboard plays an important role in that it introduces the Yankee to the Cracker and quickly establishes the fact that the two have much in common although their customs differ. The native Floridian may offer specious replies to what he considers oversimple questions, but he is likely to be puzzled at the abysmal ignorance that causes the Yankee to refer to orange groves as "orchards," sandspurs as "sandburs," and sandflies as "sandfleas." Neither does he see any reason to exclaim over a bullfrog chorus in February or the call of the whippoorwill at twilight in early March. In his own behalf he is fluently persuasive on the virtues of his particular locality; but the Yankee in Florida has become a roving visitor determined to see the entire State regardless of regional blandishments.

The first-time visitor is primarily a sightseer. He is the principal customer for the admission places along the road. He learns very soon how far Florida is supposed to project from the Old South by the discovery that a turpentine still with its Negro quarters has been turned into a tourist at traction and advertised as a survival of bygone plantation days.

Clockwise and counterclockwise the sightseeing newcomer makes the circuit of the State, filling the highways with a stream of two-way traffic. If traveling southward by the Gulf coast route, he stops to partake of a Spanish dinner in the Latin quarter of Tampa, to sit on the green benches of St. Petersburg, to view the Ringling Circus animals and art museum at Sarasota, to admire the royal palms at Fort Myers. Thence be follows the Tamiami Trail through the ghostly scrub cypress and primitive silence of the Everglades, to encounter at last the theatrical sophistication of Miami. As a side trip from the latter city, he may proceed down the long overseas highway to Key West, once the State's most populous city and an important defense base, but since its recent rehabilitation by the Federal Government something of a public curiosity, a place favored by artists and writers, and noted for its green-turtle steaks.

On his return up the Atlantic coast, the traveler may concede that publicity word-pictures of the resorts from Miami Beach northward have not been greatly exaggerated, but he is impressed by the long intervening stretches of woodland, suggesting that Florida is still very largely an empty State. From Palm Beach, which has long been the earthly Valhalla of financial achievement, he may detour inland to discover the hidden winter-vegetable kingdom on the muck lands along the southern shore of Lake Okeechobee, where Negro workers harvest thousands of carloads of beans and other fresh food supplies; or farther north he may swing inland by way of Orlando, through the great citrus groves of the hilly lake region and the thriving strawberry country around Plant City; then up to Ocala, where he can look through the glass bottoms of boats at water life in the depths of crystal-clear springs. Returning to the east coast, he inspects the far-famed natural speedway at Daytona Beach and the old Spanish fort at St. Augustine before he reaches the northern terminal city of Jacksonville. Frequently at the end of the tour, the visitor announces that he is never coming back.

His second excursion into Florida is somewhat different. On his first trip, unconsciously or deliberately, he had selected a spot where he thought later on he might want to live and play, and when he comes again he usually returns to that chosen place for a season. Ultimately, in many cases, he buys or builds a home there and becomes by slow degrees a citizen and a critic.

The evolution of a tourist into a permanent resident consists of a struggle to harmonize misconceptions and preconceptions of Florida with reality. An initial diversion is to mail northward snapshots of himself reclining under a coconut palm or a beach umbrella, with the hope that they will be delivered in the midst of a blizzard. At the same time, the tourist checks weather reports from the North, and if his home community is having a mild winter he feels that his Florida trip has been in part a swindle. Nothing short of ten-foot snowdrifts and burst waterpipes at home can make his stay in the Southland happy and complete. On the other hand, he is firmly convinced that with his departure in the spring the State folds up and the inhabitants sizzle under a pitiless sun until he gets back, official weather reports and chamber-of-commerce protests to the contrary. Eventually he takes a chance on a Florida summer and makes the discovery that the average summer temperature in Florida is lower than in North; he tries to tell about it at home, and for his pains receives a round of Bronx cheers. He is now in the agonies of transition, suspected by friends and shunned by strangers. His visits to Florida thereafter shift to visits back home, and these latter become less frequent; but "back home" has left an indelible imprint, which he proposes to stamp on Florida.

An expansive mood is one of the most familiar and sometimes costly first responses to a Florida winter sun. The person noted for taciturnity in his home community often becomes loquacious, determined that those about him shall know that he is a man of substance. This frequently makes him an easy prey to ancient confidence games; sometimes leads to unpremeditated matrimony; and almost inevitably results in the acquisition of superfluous building lots.

Already something of a solipsist, he becomes an incurable nonconformist, vigorously defending his adopted State and indignantly decrying it by turns. He refutes the tradition that life in the South is a lackadaisical existence adapted to an enervating climate. He comes here to play and to relax but at the slightest provocation he resumes his business or profession, if for no other reason than to demonstrate that the sound economic practices of his home State will pull Florida out of the doldrums he perceives it to be in. If he opens a shop, the back-home instinct is likely to reassert in choosing a name, so that Florida abounds in Michigan groceries, Maryland restaurants, Ohio dry-cleaners, Indiana laundries, and New York shoe shops.

We asked hundreds of retired people who have made new homes and a fresh start in Florida all about their experiences there. Their answers to our questions are the basis for this book.

The people we queried have been salesmen, teachers, farmers, army officers, ministers, newspapermen, advertising executives, doctors, architects, artists, railroad agents, boat builders, company presidents and firemen . . . and a lot of other things. They came to Florida from twenty-seven states.

They told us what they liked about their section of Florida and what they didn't like about it. (Forty-six percent said there wasn't *anything* they didn't like about it.)

They told us what physical ailments had diminished or disappeared in Florida, and whether they had fewer colds.

They told us how they moved their household goods, and whether the method was satisfactory. And they listed things that are better left in the North than moved.

They told us how much ready cash a couple should have to move to Florida, and how much steady income.

They told us so much about so many things that they are certainly co-authors. On some points they disagreed, but on one point they were unanimous: Florida is unrivaled as a place to make a new life.

The first reason for making a fresh start and living your new lifetime in Florida is the climate. Its pleasantness is not exaggerated. It is a gentle climate, kind to older people and literally rejuvenating. The sun really does shine most of the time, and soaks into your bones most blissfully. There are differences in temperature from north to south Florida, and differences in humidity from coastal areas to the central ridge section. Choose the spot that suits your tastes and health best.

The second reason is the number of people there like you who will become your friends and share your interests. Almost one hundred per cent of our Florida advisors say that it is easier to make friends where they are living in Florida than where they lived in the north. In Florida you won't begin to feel lonesome because you're the only person in your neighborhood who doesn't have a job to go to during the day. Rather, your retirement will be a catalyst to bring you in contact with scores of others who are retired. (And, inciden-

tally, you will be visited by a substantial number of friends and relatives from the north. Better than 99 percent of our Florida contacts said that such was the case with them.)

A third reason that Florida is a good fresh-starting place is that it is different from northern states. The living there is more informal, slower paced, and to a greater degree out of doors. You will dress entirely differently. If you have half a mind to, you will find a lot of new interests in life.

A fourth reason—unless you are wealthy—is that it costs less to live in Florida. Your biggest savings will be in fuel bills, clothing bills, and probably doctor bills.

A fifth reason is that Florida is far off—and there is no substitute for distance in getting away from business.

BEACHCOMBERS
Seagulls and tourists comb the beach on Siesta Key after the tide goes out. (Photograph © Lynn M. Stone)

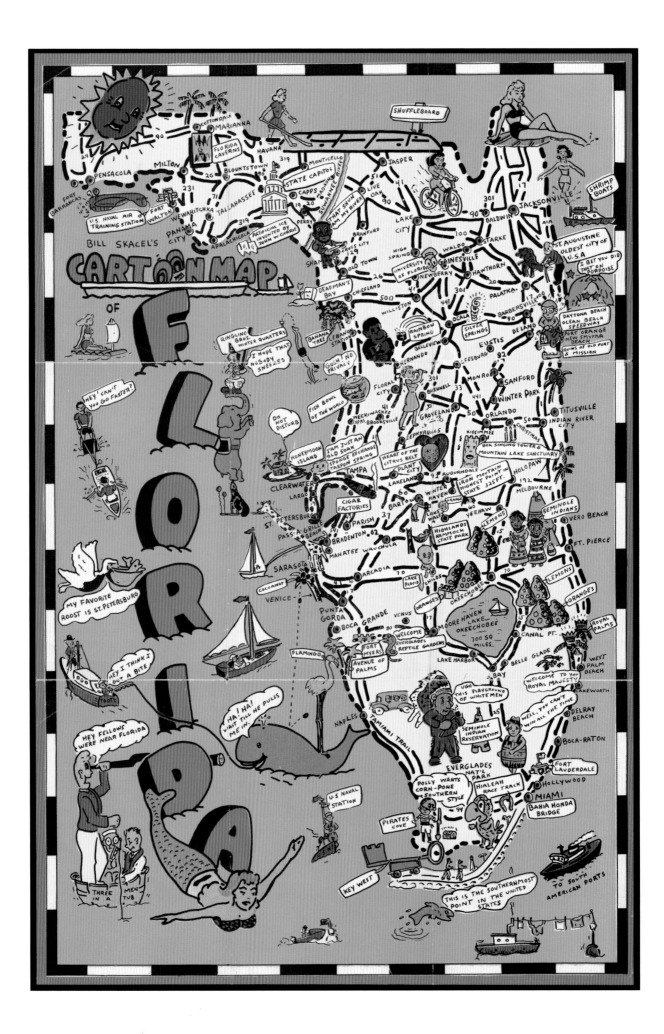

The Walt "You Will Have Fun" Disney World Themed Shopping Complex and Resort Compound

By Dave Barry

Dave Barry is funny. Whether it's through his Pulitzer Prize-winning, syndicated column for the *Miami Herald* or any of his numerous books, Barry has become one of the best known humorists in the United States today.

Barry's brand of humor is a raucous mix of silliness and over-the-top farce that often results from pointing out the absurd in everyday life. Among his most beloved books are *Dave Barry's Complete Guide to Guys* (1995), *Dave Barry is From Mars and Venus* (1997), and *Dave Barry Turns 50* (1998).

This excerpt comes from *Dave Barry's Only Travel Guide You'll Ever Need* (1991), which includes this handy guide to Disney World.

CARTOON MAP OF FLORIDA
Wooing tourists to the Florida peninsula was the goal of this cartoon map from the 1930s or 1940s.

I'M AN EXPERT on visiting Disney World, because we live only four hours away, and according to my records we spend about three-fifths of our after-tax income there. Not that I'm complaining. You can't have a bad time at Disney World. It's not *allowed.* They have hidden electronic surveillance cameras everywhere, and if they catch you failing to laugh with childlike wonder, they lock you inside a costume representing a beloved Disney character such as Goofy and make you walk about in the Florida heat getting grabbed and leaped on by violently excited children until you have learned your lesson. Yes, Disney World is a "dream vacation," and here are some tips to help make it "come true" for you!

When to Go: The best time to go, if you want to avoid huge crowds, is 1962.

How to Get There: It's possible to fly, but if you want the total Disney World experience, you should drive there with a minimum of four hostile children via the longest possible route. If you live in Georgia, for example, you should plan a route that includes Oklahoma.

Once you get to Florida, you can't miss Disney World, because the Disney corporation owns the entire center of the state. Just get on any major highway, and eventually it will dead-end in a Disney parking area large enough to have its own climate, populated by large nomadic families who have been trying to find their cars since the Carter administration. Be sure to note carefully where you leave your car, because later on you may want to sell it so you can pay for your admission tickets.

But never mind the price; the point is that now you're finally *there*, in the ultimate vacation fantasy paradise, ready to have fun! Well, okay, you're not exactly there *yet*. First you have to wait for the parking-lot tram, driven by cheerful uniformed Disney employees, to come around and pick you up and give you a helpful lecture about basic tram-safety rules such as never fall out of the tram without coming to a full and complete stop.

But now the tram ride is over and it's time for fun! Right? Don't be an idiot. It's time to wait in line to buy admission tickets. Most experts recommend that you go with the 47-day pass, which will give you a chance, if you never eat or sleep, to visit *all* of the Disney themed attractions, including The City of the Future, The Land of Yesterday, The Dull Suburban Residential Community of Sometime Next Month,

AQUA-BLUE WATERS
The warm, clear, aqua-blue color of the Gulf waters beckons sunbathers at Seaside. (Photograph © Robb Helfrick)

Wet Adventure, Farms on Mars, The World of Furniture, Sponge Encounter, the Nuclear Flute Orchestra, Appliance Island, and the Great Underwater Robot Hairdresser Adventure, to name just a few.

Okay, you've taken out a second mortgage and purchased your tickets! Now, finally, it's time to . . . wait in line again! This time, it's for the monorail, a modern, futuristic transportation system that whisks you to the Magic Kingdom at nearly half the speed of a lawn tractor. Along the way cheerful uniformed Disney World employees will offer you some helpful monorail-safety tips such as never set fire to the monorail without first removing your personal belongings.

And now, at last, you're at the entrance to the Magic Kingdom itself! No more waiting in line for transportation! It's time to *wait in line to get in.* Wow! Look at all the *other* people waiting to get in! There are tour groups here with names like "Entire Population of Indiana." There sure must be some great attractions inside these gates!

And now you've inched your way to the front of the line, and the cheerful uniformed Disney employee is stamping your hand with a special invisible chemical that penetrates your nervous system and causes you to temporarily acquire the personality of a cow. "Moo!" you shout as you surge forward with the rest of the herd.

And now, unbelievably, you're actually inside the Magic Kingdom! At last! Mecca! You crane your head to see over the crowd around you, and with innocent childlike wonder you behold: *a much larger crowd.* Ha ha! You are having some kind of fun now!

And now you are pushing your way forward,

SPACE
Tourists flock to watch the launch of the space shuttle Discovery *from the Lighthouse Landing Restaurant at Daytona Beach. The Kennedy Space Center on Merritt Island and the Cape Canaveral Air Force Station are ground zero for the United States's space program, attracting thousands of tourists annually to the space museum, visitor center, IMAX theater, astronaut memorial, and launching pad. (Photograph © Tony Arruza)*

GATOR CHIC
Alligators have long been a symbol attracting tourists to Florida. This smattering of gator-chic postcards from the 1930s through the 1960s chronicles the tourist's strange love affair with the Florida reptile.

WRESTLING ALLIGATOR UNDER WATER AT SILVER SPRINGS

DIVERS
Snorkelers explore Alexander Springs in the Ocala National Forest. (Photograph © Tony Arruza)

thrusting other vacationers aside, knocking over their strollers if necessary, because little Jason wants to ride on Space Mountain. Little Jason has been talking about Space Mountain ever since Oklahoma, and by God you're going to take him on it, no matter how long the . . . My God! Can *this* be the line for Space Mountain? This line is so long that there are Cro-Magnon families at the front! Perhaps if you explain to little Jason that he could be a deceased old man by the time he gets on the actual ride, he'll agree to skip it and . . . NO! Don't scream, little Jason! We'll just purchase some official Mickey Mouse sleeping bags, and we'll stay in line as long as it takes! The hell with third grade! We'll just stand here and chew our cuds! Mooooo!

Speaking of education, you should be sure to visit Epcot Center, which features exhibits sponsored by large corporations showing you how various challenges facing the human race are being met and overcome thanks to the selfless efforts of large corporations. Epcot Center also features pavilions built by various foreign nations, where you can experience an extremely realistic simulation of what life in these nations would be like if they consisted almost entirely of restaurants and souvenir stores.

One memorable Epcot night my family and I ate at the German restaurant, where I had several large beers and a traditional German delicacy called "Bloatwurst," which is a sausage that can either be eaten or used as a tackling dummy. When we got out I felt like one of those snakes that eat a cow whole and then just lie around and digest it for a couple of months. But my son was determined to go on a new educational Epcot ride called "The Body," wherein you sit in a compartment that simulates what it would be like if you got inside a spaceship-like vehicle and got shrunk down to the size of a gnat and got injected inside a person's body.

I'll tell you what it's like: awful. You're looking at a screen showing an extremely vivid animated simulation of the human interior, which is not the most appealing way to look at a human unless you're attracted to white blood cells the size of motor homes. Meanwhile the entire compartment is bouncing you around violently, especially when you go through the aorta. "Never go through the aorta after eating German food," that is my new travel motto.

What gets me is, I waited in line for an *hour* to do this. I could have experienced essentially the same level

of enjoyment merely by sticking my finger down my throat.

Which brings me to my idea for getting rich. No doubt you have noted that, in most amusement parks, the popularity of a ride is directly proportional to how horrible it is. There's hardly ever a line for nice, relaxing rides like the merry-go-round. But there will always be a huge crowd, mainly consisting of teenagers, waiting to go on a ride with a name like "The Dicer," where they strap people into what is essentially a giant food processor and turn it on and then phone the paramedics.

So my idea is to open up a theme park called "Dave World," which will have a ride called "The Fall of Death." This will basically be a 250-foot tower. The way it will work is, you climb to the top, a trapdoor opens up, and you splat onto the asphalt below like a bushel of late-summer tomatoes.

Obviously, for legal reasons, I couldn't let anybody actually go on this ride. There would be a big sign that said:

WARNING!

NOBODY CAN GO ON THIS RIDE.
THIS RIDE IS INVARIABLY FATAL,

THANK YOU.

But this would only make The Fall of Death more popular. Every teenager in the immediate state would come to Dave World just to stand in line for it.

Dave World would also have an attraction called "ParentLand," which would have a sign outside that said: "Sorry, Kids! This Attraction Is for Mom 'n' Dad Only!" Inside would be a bar. For younger children, there would be "Soil Fantasy," a themed play area consisting of dirt or, as a special "rainy-day" bonus, mud.

I frankly can't see how Dave World could fail to become a huge financial success that would make me rich and enable me to spend the rest of my days traveling the world with my family. So the hell with it.

❧

Seeing Other Attractions in the Disney World Area
You must be very careful here. You must sneak out of Disney World in the dead of night, because the Disney people do *not* want you leaving the compound and spending money elsewhere. If they discover that you're

gone, cheerful uniformed employees led by Mickey Mouse's lovable dog Pluto, who will sniff the ground in a comical manner, will track you down. And when they catch you, it's *into the Goofy suit.*

So we're talking about a major risk, but it's worth it for some of the attractions around Disney World. The two best ones, as it happens, are right next to each other near a town called Kissimmee. One of them is the world headquarters of the Tupperware company, where you can take a guided tour that includes a Historic Food Containers Museum. I am not making this up.

I am also not making up Gatorland, which is next door. After entering Gatorland through a giant pair of pretend alligator jaws, you find yourself on walkways over a series of murky pools in which are floating a large number of alligators that appear to be recovering from severe hangovers, in the sense that they hardly ever move. You can purchase fish to feed them, but the typical Gatorland alligator will ignore a fish even if it lands directly on its head. Sometimes you'll see an alligator, looking bored, wearing three or four rotting, fly-encrusted fish, like some kind of High Swamp Fashion headgear.

This is very entertaining, of course, but the *real* action at Gatorland, the event that brings even the alligators to life, is the Assault on the Dead Chickens, which is technically known as the Gator Jumparoo. I am also not making this up. The way it works is, a large crowd of tourists gathers around a central pool, over which, suspended from wires, are a number of plucked headless chicken carcasses. As the crowd, encouraged by the Gatorland announcer, cheers wildly, the alligators lunge out of the water and rip the chicken carcasses down with their jaws. Once you've witnessed this impressive event, you will never again wonder how America got to be the country that it is today.

GRAND HOTEL
The grand hotels of Miami Beach inspired awe from tourists and retirees alike. This image of the glamorous Roney Plaza Hotel was taken in 1939 by famed photographer Marion Post Wolcott. (Library of Congress)

Miami
Downtown Miami glows like a tiara of jewels at sunset. (Photograph © Doug Perrine/Innerspace Visions)

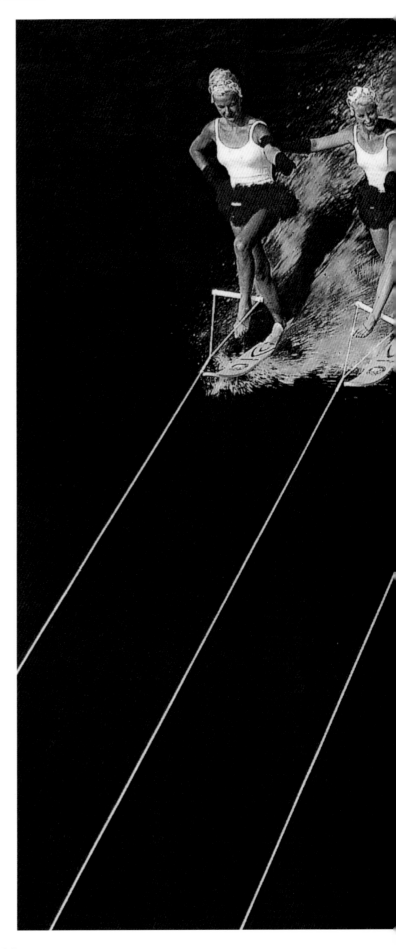

WATER-SKI BALLET
With their tutus waving in the breeze, a formation of water-skiing ballerinas strut their stuff at Cypress Gardens in the 1960s.

CHAPTER 5

The Once and Future Land

"Golden sunshine adds golden years."
—Miami tourist poster, 1920s

Florida reinvents itself daily. With a stream of new citizens, immigrants, refugees, and vacationers and with never-ending growth and development, the Sunshine State is in constant flux.

What the future holds for the state is impossible to predict. One of Florida's challenges will be to age gracefully without forgetting its past, traditions, and natural history.

ABOVE: AUDUBON PAINTING OF A ROSEATE SPOONBILL
John James Audubon's painting of a roseate spoonbill gleams with the colors of the bird's brilliant plumage.

OPPOSITE PAGE: NATURAL BEAUTY
Just another Florida sunset, as the clouds above Captiva Island catch the last rays of the day's sun. (Photograph © Henry H. Holdsworth)

Spared Angola

By Virgil Suárez

Born in Havana, Cuba, Virgil Suárez has made his home in Florida like many Cubanos. Cuban-Americans in Florida have created whole new lives for themselves in their adopted land, and over the last forty years have thoroughly transformed everything in the state from food to politics. Some, like Suárez, have also altered the literary landscape.

A novelist, poet, and editor, Suárez has published three novels, *Latin Jazz* (1989), *Havana Thursdays* (1995), and *Going Under* (1996) as well as the collection of stories *Welcome to the Oasis* (1992). In addition, he has edited several anthologies of Latino writers such as *Iguana Dreams* (1992) and *Little Havana Blues* (1996).

This excerpt comes from his inventive collection of autobiographical poems and stories that make up his memoir *Spared Angola: Memories From a Cuban-American Childhood* (1997). "Angola" refers to the conscription of Cuban youths to fight in the Angolan revolution; Suárez was spared this experience when his parents took him into exile.

AFTER A TWENTY-YEAR absence, my grandmother, Donatila, flies from Havana to Miami for a visit. Waiting for her in the crowded and noisy lobby of Miami International Airport, I am struck by memories of my childhood in the arms of this woman who, except for vague moments, is a perfect stranger. To my mother she is Tina of the constant aches and headaches, of the bouts with rheumatism, of the skin disease that spotted her face and neck with pink blotches, of the hair the color of smoke and straw. *Abuela* Tina. Twenty years before this moment caught in the restless humdrum of waiting, this woman about to visit showed me many things: how to feed leftover rice to chickens, tie my shoelaces, brew the kind of watery coffee I like to drink with toasted bread. She kept my behind from feeling the wrath of my father's belt on numerous occasions; she stayed with me while I took a shower in the room by the side of the clapboard house because I was terrified of the bullfrogs that sought the humidity trapped there. She told me stories, most of which I've forgotten, except for the one about the old hag who would wait for a man to come by on horseback to cross the old bridge. The hag would jump on the horse and spook the animal and the rider. The horsemen knew never to look back or risk spooking themselves crazy. "Never look back," she said, "as you cross your bridges." The flight arrives and the waiting intensifies. My mother sinks her nails into my flesh as she holds my hand. My father every so often retrieves a handkerchief from his back pocket (he's never used one) and wipes his forehead and under his eyes. The first few passengers come out the glass doors of Customs and are greeted by relatives who have never forgotten these tired and worn faces, frail bodies. Parents, sisters, brothers, sons, daughters, all now looking thirty-six years older. "Time," my father says, "is a son

of a bitch." Finally, I spot my aunt (I have not seen her for as long as I have not seen my grandmother), my father's sister who'd gotten cancer. She is holding on to my grandmother, and I realize my memory has served me better than I am willing to admit. Grandmother Tina looks the same except for the patches of the skin disease which have completely taken over her face. My mother screams and lets go of my hand and runs to the arms of her mother. My father to his sister. I stand back and brace myself. After the hugs and the kisses, my mother says, "There he is! Your grandson, Mama!" She walks toward me and I find I cannot move, for I cannot believe in movement; I am still stuck in time. She comes toward me. "*¿No te acuerdas de mí?*" she says, her Spanish the necessary tug. I lean into her arms, for she is small and frail, and we stand there in the middle of the lobby. I tell her that I do remember. I remember everything. Slowly now we make our way out of the terminal to the parking lot, into the car, onto the freeway, home to my parents', up the stairs and into the living room of an apartment in which I've spent so very little time. All this time everybody has been talking except me; I've been driving and listening, bewildered by all the catching up. In the living room now, waiting for refreshments, my grandmother comes over to where I sit and she holds my face between her hands. She looks into my eyes. Can I? Can I remember this woman? My grandmother Donatila. She's an apparition, I think, but don't say it. She says, "You must tell me about you, all that the distance has taken from us." I tell her I am happy to see her, after so much time. "*¿Sabes?*" she says. "You are a lucky young man. Your parents did the right thing. When they took you out of Cuba, your parents spared you. Yes, you were spared. Spared Angola."

PONCE DE LÉON INLET LIGHTHOUSE
The first-order Fresnel lamp high atop the 168-foot-tall Ponce de Léon Inlet lighthouse at Daytona Beach was first lit in 1887. After faithfully serving mariners for decades, the U.S. Coast Guard decommissioned the light in 1970 and built a basic steel-tower beacon at Smyrna Dunes to replace it. In an odd twist of fate, urban development saved the venerable lighthouse. When high-rise construction blocked shippers' view of the new Smyrna Dunes light, the Coast Guard relit the Ponce de Léon Inlet lighthouse in 1983 with an aeromarine beacon. (Photograph © Tony Arruza)

***ABOVE:* FLORIDA SUNSET**
Florida is justly famous for its sunsets. (Photographs © Lynn M. Stone)

***RIGHT:* PEANUT VENDOR**
A street vendor offers boiled and roasted peanuts—as well as a diversity of other items including state, national, and college flags—from his trailer in Quincy. (Photograph © Tony Arruza)

***OPPOSITE PAGE:* FLAMENCO**
Florida's Spanish past lives on in the rhythms and fire of flamenco at Columbia Restaurant in Ybor City. (Photograph © Tony Arruza)

The Agüero Sisters

By Cristina García

Cristina García was born in Havana, Cuba, but grew up in New York City. She served as a *Time* magazine correspondent in Miami, New York City, and Los Angeles, before turning her hand to writing novels infused by her own past.

Her first book, the tour de force novel *Dreaming in Cuban* (1992), was nominated for a National Book Award, was widely translated throughout the world, and has become a classic of modern Latino fiction.

García's most recent novel, *The Agüero Sisters* (1997), examines the lives of two sisters broken apart by the Cuban Revolution. One sister, Reina, still lives in Cuba and struggles with her faith in *la Revolución*. The other, Constancia, is exiled in the land of the American Dream. But even in her retirement in Florida, Constancia is haunted by memories of her homeland, as this beautifully crafted excerpt details.

❧

CONSTANCIA AGÜERO CRUZ considers the illumined corpse of her father-in-law at the foot of the altar rail. Arturo Cruz's face is overly rouged, and his hands, enlaced with a worn wooden rosary, appear stiff and squared-tipped as piano keys. His family and friends, spent by the upheaval of his death, are gathered in the front pews. Constancia adjusts her veiled hat, smooths the sash of her black chiffon dress. Against the back wall of the chancel, a dominion of faded saints hovers with long-forgotten ecstasies.

Dusk erupts through the stained-glass windows of the church. The candles gutter as if disturbed by a draft. Constancia is startled. In the tropics, twilight is such a swift affair, one flamboyant cloak exchanged for another, with a flare and a whirl. In New York City, she recalls wistfully, the days receded gradually, sulking for hours.

"It is a season of ruin, a season of salvation." Constancia ignores the pouchy-eyed priest, the irksome hymns prescribed for grief. Her father-in-law died from a surge of blood that flooded his brain during a game of dominoes at Gerardo's *carnicería*. Constancia doesn't question his passing. There are, she knows, reasons good enough for everything that happens.

Maldición, maldición, maldición. Constancia imagines the words colliding along the stone floor, rattling the coffin and the narcissistic saints. She reaches for her husband's hand. It is cold and fleshy. Heberto has been irascible for weeks, is worse now that his father is dead. The family was close back in Cuba, before debt and exile drove them apart. Now Constancia fears that Heberto, too, will choose to die, like the aborigines who paint their faces and disappear into the forest when their time comes.

From a nearby pew, her first husband, Gonzalo Cruz scrapes his way to his father's coffin on his flame-tree cane. Constancia hasn't seen him in thirty-three years. It is difficult for her to reconcile the sight of this man with the memory of him, with the despair that corrupted her for any other love.

Gonzalo's left leg is shorter than his right, a souvenir of the Bay of Pigs. When Constancia knew him, there was no limp. His legs were his best feature then, muscular and smooth as a boy's. Still, something of his old rapacity lurks in his wilted bearing, in his fading marauder's face. Constancia wonders, shrewdly assessing her ex-husband, if this is what their son will

look like at sixty.

Relatives have informed her that Gonzalo Cruz is slowly dying. His malady yellows his skin to a delicate tarnish, as if privileged by the sun, and he exudes a potent, beckoning odor. From his eleventh-floor suite at the Good Samaritan Hospital, Gonzalo holds court like a deposed dictator, with every manner of refugee and sycophant. He is pleased when he is caught, as happens frequently, in flagrante delicto.

Constancia considers what her daughter told her over the phone last week. That doctors today know what will kill you by the time you are thirty-five. There are magnetic resonance imaging machines, Isabel said, that spit out cross-sections of the human torso, pinpointing the petrified specks that ultimately signal death. "We are *all*," she stressed, "radiant with disease."

Isabel is two months pregnant. She's been living on Oahu for the past year with her painter boyfriend, Austin Feck. She makes oddly shaped objects from clay, fires them in the Japanese manner. Girl or boy, married or not, Isabel and her boyfriend plan to name their baby Raku. Constancia isn't ready to be a grandmother yet, but she plots, during the countless minute deliberations of her day, how she can wrest this child, her first grandchild, from its undeserved fate.

Recently, Constancia received a catalogue of Austin's latest exhibit, *Images of Isabel*. Her daughter's face, her naked body, whole or in select close-ups, floating in a strange, distorting light. Constancia blanched to look at them, the glossy, vulnerable pinks of Isabel's private parts. Her daughter says she plans to continue modeling for Austin throughout her pregnancy, all the more now since she's stopped throwing clay. She fears that the lead in her glazes might harm their unborn child.

It's dark by the time they reach the cemetery. Constancia has never heard of a nighttime burial, but her father-in-law left a will with specific instructions. Everyone lights white tapers from a tiki torch, then slowly circles the funeral tent. Two clarinetists in black tie play a tune Constancia doesn't recognize. Arturo Cruz's longtime mistress, Jacinta Fuentes, all ruddy bulk, with pearls the size of tamarinds, tries to leap into her lover's grave but is restrained by a circle of friends.

HARBOR
Fishing boats and brown pelicans await the start of day in the harbor at Placida. (Photograph © Lynn M. Stone)

The following evening, Constancia's husband announces he's going fishing in Biscayne Bay. Constancia knows that Heberto will return at dawn without a single fish. One night, he'll pledge to bring home a catch of red snapper; the next, a dozen sea bass for a bouillabaisse. Heberto keeps up with the fishing reports: this school of marlin moving offshore in unfathomable numbers; a swordfish the size of a man recently caught in the Gulf Stream. Constancia imagines her husband upright in his little motorboat, addressing the sky in his earnest, formal manner. She's convinced that he doesn't even bother to drop his line.

How different Heberto is from his younger brother. The two of them lie continually, congenitally, but Heberto's lies are more innocent, a quiet, wistful habit. Gonzalo's lies were blatant and unapologetic, inaccurate as language itself. In fact, Constancia could accuse Gonzalo of only two straightforward acts during their marriage: impregnating her, then leaving her when he found out. In all these years, he has never set eyes on their son, Silvestre, deaf from the time he was four. Another casualty of that *dichosa* revolution.

It is the last day of January. Constancia, folds a sheet of stationery in half and slips in a pair of hundred-dollar bills for her son. Silvestre used to reproach her for sending him cash, but he no longer acknowledges the monthly supplement. Constancia doesn't know whether he saves it or spends it or throws it away. It doesn't matter anyway. The money, she realized a long time ago, is more for her than for him.

Constancia keeps a large store of high-denomination bills hidden in the false bottom of her traveling vanity case and in a secret account at a local Nicaraguan bank. She siphoned the money from the tobacco store in the last months before it was sold. She thought it prudent to hoard the stash for unexpected plans. Surprisingly, Heberto didn't miss the cash.

ART DECO COOL
Miami Beach's famed Art Deco National Historic District encom-passes some 800 buildings along eighty blocks in South Beach. Cream-colored facades highlighted with chic pastel colors and streamlined design dating to the 1930s typify the myriad hotels, apartment buildings, restaurants, and storefronts in the neighborhood. In 1979, the district became the first neighborhood featuring twentieth-century buildings to be added to the National Register of Historic Places. (Photograph © Robb Helfrick)

The lights parade in the sliding glass doors of her balcony, aimed at the sea. The sky is muddy with low-hanging clouds. Constancia imagines the tops of the palm trees piercing the soft masses, drinking in the purity above. Tonight she is grateful for the moon's absence. Without a moon and with the sea nearby, she can lose herself in the night's imprecisions.

In the pool below, a wrinkled woman swims with a snorkel mask and fins. What could she be searching for at this hour in the concrete blue?

Constancia goes to the kitchen and heats a plate of rice, cooks a yam to bulging in the microwave. Her slacks are getting a little snug, her espadrilles too. She's gained three and a half pounds since she arrived in Florida. Her acquaintances at the yacht club tell her the extra weight becomes her. But Constancia doesn't believe these women. She knows she isn't one of them, that her life outside Miami will always mark her as a foreigner.

The problem, Constancia decided, is that the *cubanas* here can't make comfortable assumptions about her. One of them, a socialite named Rosalina Bellaire de Lavigna, asked her where she'd had her face "done." Rosalina was skeptical when Constancia vowed she hadn't undergone surgery. Another time, Constancia mentioned she'd voted Democratic (just once, for Jimmy Carter), and the room fell starkly silent. How could she possibly define herself by such unambiguous terms?

Constancia doesn't consider herself an exile in the same way as many of the Cubans here. In fact, she shuns their habit of fierce nostalgia, their trafficking in the past like exaggerating peddlers. *Her* father was a scientist, concerned with the biological exigencies of origin and barter. Evolution, Papi told her again and again, is more precise than history. Who, then, could pretend to the answers?

Of course, she wouldn't dare say this aloud in Miami and expect to survive.

Constancia moved to Key Biscayne just before the new year. She decorated her apartment all in white from a close-out furniture sale at Burdine's. She's thought of getting a job in sales—Avon has an opening for a district manager—but Heberto has persuaded her to wait until they're more settled. Constancia misses her work, but there is something more. Miami is disconcerting to her, an inescapable culture shock, the air thickly charged with expiring dreams.

The light is blinding too, a sentence to the past, to her life in Cuba. Everywhere, there is a mass of disquieting details. The deep-fried croquettes for sale on the corner. The accent of the valet who parks her car. Her seamstress's old-fashioned stitching. And the songs, slow as regret, on the afternoon radio.

At the best *bodega* in Little Havana, two dozen varieties of bananas are sold. There are pyramids of juicy mangoes, soursops, custard apples, and papayas. In a flash, they'll make her a milk shake that tastes of her past. Every Friday, Constancia loads up her pink Cadillac convertible with fresh fruit to purée and cries all the way home.

Constancia remembers the time she accompanied her father to the central market in Havana. Mama was already dead by then. She and Papi wandered around for hours, surrendering themselves to a thousand aromas. Her father loved the poultry stalls best, squawking with barnyard fowl and the more delicate clamor of pheasants, partridges, and quail. She preferred the fish vendors' displays—giant Morro crabs, toothy parrot fish, oysters, eels, and always a few good-sized sharks—perhaps because when she was a child in Camagüey, the ocean had seemed so far away.

SEA TURTLE
A loggerhead turtle hatchling makes its way from its nest on Juno Beach to dive into the ocean and begin its life at sea. (Photograph © Doug Perrine/Innerspace Visions)

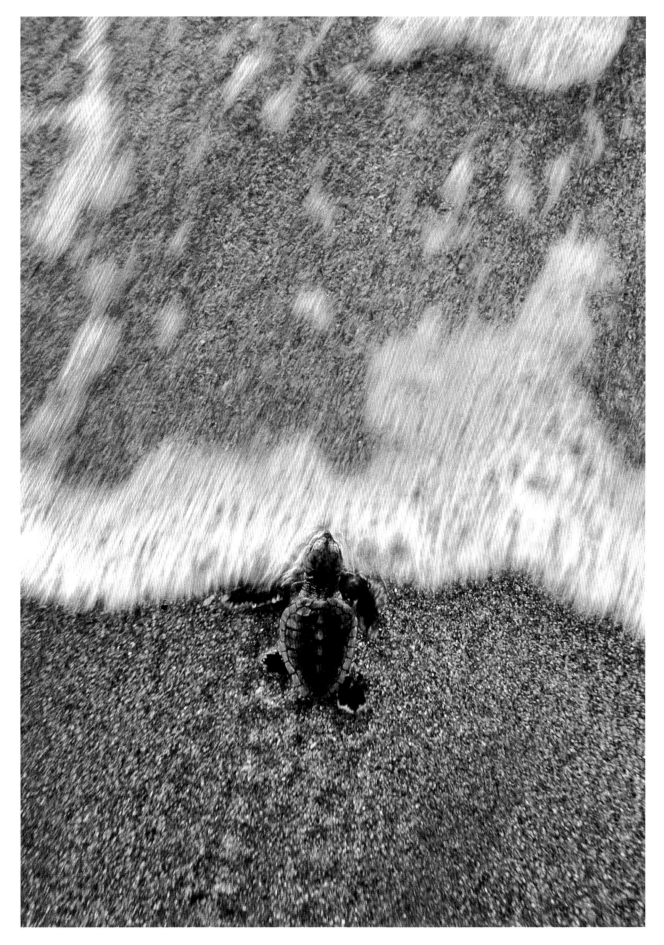

Cross Creek

By Marjorie Kinnan Rawlings

For Marjorie Kinnan Rawlings, Florida was a land of spiritual rebirth and boundless springs of inspiration. In 1928, she moved from her native Washington, D. C., to a farm at Cross Creek near Gainesville. There, the land, the water, and most of all, the people infused her with renewed faith in the world.

A longtime journalist, she began publishing short stories about her newfound home in *Scribner's* magazine in the 1930s. In 1938, she published her now-famous novel about Florida, *The Yearling*, which won the 1939 Pulitzer Prize for Fiction.

Rawlings also wrote nonfiction with great passion, writing of the farm families and her other central Florida neighbors in her memoir *Cross Creek*. Published in 1942, the book became a beloved addition to many Floridians' sense of tradition and history.

SUNRISE
Dawn makes its way through the morning mist in a Florida oak stand. (Photograph © Lynn M. Stone)

Cross Creek is a bend in a country road, by land, and the flowing of Lochloosa Lake into Orange Lake, by water. We are four miles west of the small village of Island Grove, nine miles east of a turpentine still, and on the other sides we do not count distance at all, for the two lakes and the broad marshes create an infinite space between us and the horizon. We are five white families; "Old Boss" Brice, the Glissons, the Mackays and the Bernie Basses; and two colored families, Henry Woodward and the Mickenses. People in Island Grove consider us just a little biggety and more than a little queer. Black Kate and I between us once misplaced some household object, quite unreasonably.

I said, "Kate, am I crazy, or are you?"

She gave me her quick sideways glance that was never entirely impudent.

"Likely all two of us. Don't you reckon it take somebody a little bit crazy to live out here at the Creek?"

At one time or another most of us at the Creek have been suspected of a degree of madness. Madness is only a variety of mental nonconformity and we are all individualists here. I am reminded of Miss Malin and the Cardinal in the Gothic tale, "The Deluge at Norderney."

"But are you not," said the Cardinal, "a little——"

"Mad?" asked the old lady. "I thought that you were aware of that, My Lord."

The Creek folk of color are less suspect than the rest of us. Yet there is something a little different about them from blacks who live gregariously in Quarters, so that even if they did not live at the Creek, they would stay, I think, somehow aloof from the layer-cake life of the average Negro. Tom Glisson and Old Boss and I think anybody is crazy not to live here, but I know what Kate meant. We have chosen a deliberate isolation, and are enamored of it, so that to the sociable we give the feeling that St. Simeon Stylites on top of his desert pillar must have given the folk who begged him to come down and live among them. He liked the pillar or he would not have been there. Something about it suited his nature. And something about Cross Creek suits us—or something about us makes us cling to it contentedly, lovingly and often in exasperation, through the vicissitudes that have driven others away.

"I wouldn't live any place else," Tom said, "if I had gold buried in Georgia. I tell you, so much happens at Cross Creek."

There is of course an affinity between people and places. "And God called the dry land Earth; and the gathering together of waters called He Seas; and God saw that it was good." This was before man, and if there be such a thing as racial memory, the consciousness of land and water must lie deeper in the core of us than any knowledge of our fellow beings. We were bred of earth before we were born of our mothers. Once born, we can live without mother or father, or any other kin, or any friend, or any human love. We cannot live without the earth or apart from it, and something is shrivelled in a man's heart when he turns away from it and concerns himself only with the affairs of men.

And along with our deep knowledge of the earth is a preference of each of us for certain different kinds of it, for the earth is various as we are various. One man longs for the mountains, and does not even need to have been a child of the mountains to have this longing; and another man yearns for the valleys or the plains. A seaman I know said that he was making a great effort to assure himself of going to Hell, for the Bible says that in Heaven "there shall be no more sea," and Heaven for him is a place of great waters.

We at the Creek need and have found only very simple things. We must need flowering and fruiting trees, for all of us have citrus groves of one size or another. We must need a certain blandness of season, with a longer and more beneficent heat than many require, for there is never too much sun for us, and through the long summers we do not complain. We need the song of birds, and there is none finer than the redbird. We need the sound of rain coming across the *hamaca*, and the sound of wind in trees—and there is no more sensitive Aeolian harp than the palm. The pine is good, for the needles brushing one another have a great softness, and we have the wind in the pines, too.

We need above all, I think, a certain remoteness from urban confusion, and while this can be found in other places, Cross Creek offers it with such beauty and grace that once entangled with it, no other place seems possible to us, just as when truly in love none other offers the comfort of the beloved. We are not even offended when others do not share our delight. Tom Glisson and I often laugh together at the people who consider the Creek dull, or, in the precise sense, outlandish.

MEDITATION
A gazebo full of empty deck chairs beckons travelers to stop and watch the waves. (Photograph © Eric Dusenbery/Dimensions Photography)

BARRACUDA
A great barracuda swims past the remains of the crow's nest of the U.S. Coast Guard's Duane, which sank off Key Largo. (Photograph © Doug Perrine/Innerspace Visions)

154

"There was a fellow woke me up," he said, "was lost. I'd heard his car go by and hit the Creek bridge like cattle stompeding. I wondered if any one in that big of a hurry knowed where he was going. Directly he come back and stopped and I heard him holler from the gate. I pulled on my breeches and went out to him. I said, 'Reckon you're lost.' 'Lost ain't the word for it,' he said. 'Is this the end of the world? Where in God's name am I?' I said, 'Mister, you're at Cross Creek.' 'That don't tell me a thing,' he said. 'I still ain't anywhere.'"

"People in town sometimes say to me when I start home at night," I said, "'We hate to see you drive off alone to that awful place.'"

"Well," he said comfortably, "they just don't know the Creek."

We do. We know one another. Our knowledge is a strange kind, totally without intimacy, for we go our separate ways and meet only when new fences are strung, or some one's stock intrudes on another, or

***ABOVE:* CROSS CREEK HOME**
Author Marjorie Kinnan Rawlings's home at Cross Creek was a simple Cracker cottage. As she wrote in Cross Creek, *her beloved memoir of the area, "Who owns Cross Creek? The red-birds, I think, more than I . . . we are tenants and not possessors, lovers and not masters. Cross Creek belongs to the wind and the rain, to the sun and the seasons, to the cosmic secrecy of seed, and beyond all, to time." (Photograph © Jeff Ripple)*

***RIGHT:* SUWANNEE RIVER**
Made famous in song, the Suwannee River begins as a blackwater river in Georgia's equally famous Okefenokee Swamp. The waters travel some 250 miles—running through the Big Shoals pictured here—before emptying into the Gulf of Mexico. (Photograph © Jeff Ripple)

ABOVE: THE CALL OF THE SEA
Generations of children have listened to the magical call of the sea coming from within a conch shell. (Photograph © Lynn M. Stone)

RIGHT: NEVER-ENDING WAVES
The sun rises over the Gulf waters at Grayton Beach. (Photograph © Maresa Pryor)

when one of us is ill or in trouble, or when woods fires come too close, or when a shooting occurs and we must agree who is right and who must go to jail, or when the weather is so preposterous, either as to heat or cold, or rain or drought, that we seek out excuses to be together, to talk together about the common menace. We get into violent arguments and violent quarrels, sometimes about stock, sometimes because we take sides with our favorites when the dark Mickens family goes on the warpath. The village exaggerates our differences and claims that something in the Creek water makes people quarrelsome. Our amenities pass unnoticed. We do injustices among ourselves, and another of us, not directly involved, usually manages to put in a judicious word on the side of right. The one who is wrong usually ends by admitting it, and all is well again, and I have done my share of the eating of humble pie. And when the great enemies of Old Starvation and Old Death come skulking down on us, we put up a united front and fight them side by side, as we fight the woods fires. Each of us knows the foibles of the others and the strength and the weaknesses, and who can be counted on for what. Old Aunt Martha Mickens, with her deceptive humility and her face like poured chocolate, is perhaps the shuttle that has woven our knowledge, carrying back and forth, with the apparent innocence of a nest-building bird, the most revealing bits of gossip; the sort of gossip that tells, not trivial facts, but human motives and the secrets of human hearts. Each of us pretends that she carries these threads only about others and never about us, but we all know better, and that none of us is spared.

A dozen other whites and a baker's dozen of other blacks have lived at one time or another among us, or in the immediate vicinity of the Creek, coming and going like the robins. We are clannish and do not feel the same about them as we feel about ourselves. It was believed in the beginning that I was one of these. Surely the Creek would drive me away. When it was clear that a freezing of the orange crop was as great a catastrophe to me as to the others, surely I would not be here long. It was when old Martha, who had set up the Brices as Old Boss and Old Miss, referred to me one day as Young Miss, that it was understood by all of us that I was here to stay.

For myself, the Creek satisfies a thing that had gone hungry and unfed since childhood days. I am often lonely. Who is not? But I should be lonelier in the heart of a city. And as Tom says, "So much happens here." I walk at sunset, east along the road. There are no houses in that direction, except the abandoned one where the wild plums grow, white with bloom in springtime. I usually walk halfway to the village and back again. No one goes, like myself, on foot, except Bernie Bass perhaps, striding firmly in rubber boots with his wet sack of fish over his shoulder. Sometimes black Henry passes with a mule and wagon, taking a load of lighter'd home to Old Boss; sometimes a neighbor's car, or the wagon that turns off toward the turpentine woods to collect the resin, or the timber truck coming out from the pine woods. The white folks call "Hey!" and children wave gustily and with pleasure. A stranger driving by usually slows down and asks whether I want a lift. The Negroes touch a finger to their ragged caps or pretend courteously not to see me. Evening after evening I walk as far as the magnolias near Big Hammock, and home, and see no one.

Folk call the road lonely, because there is not human traffic and human stirring. Because I have walked it so many times and seen such a tumult of life there, it seems to me one of the most populous highways of my acquaintance. I have walked it in ecstasy, and in joy it is beloved. Every pine tree, every gallberry bush, every passion vine, every joree rustling in the underbrush, is vibrant. I have walked it in trouble, and the wind in the trees beside me is easing. I have walked it in despair, and the red of the sunset is my own blood dissolving into the night's darkness. For all such things were on earth before us, and will survive after us, and it is given to us to join ourselves with them and to be comforted.